I0187830

THE WAY INTO THE FUTURE

A MARDUKITE SYSTEMOLOGY PUBLICATION

Published from
Mardukite Borsippa HQ, San Luis Valley, Colorado
Founding Church of Mardukite Zuism,
Mardukite Academy & Systemology Society

Graphic Assistance & Systemology Logos by Kyra Kaos

MARDUKITE ACADEMY OF SYSTEMOLOGY PREMIERE EDITION

THE WAY INTO THE FUTURE

A HANDBOOK FOR THE NEW HUMAN

Collected Works by Joshua Free

Edited by Publication Staff, James Thomas

ISBN : 978-0-578-92813-5

A selection of critical writings from
The Systemology Handbook
specially edited for introducing the
Mardukite Systemology Society

Premiere Hardcover Collector's Edition—July 2021

mardukite.com

Discover The Secret to Being Human...

The Way Into The Future illuminates a *Pathway* leading to a true spiritual evolution and the attainment of Planet Earth's true "metahuman" destiny.

It begins with a brief survey of the most ancient writings—the Arcane Tablets—which have shaped Human consciousness for thousands of years. Then it continues by taking a Seeker on an amazing journey of concise, practical and effective spiritual technologies; the product of a decade of underground research and discovery by Joshua Free and the Systemology Society, and which are now publicly visible for the first time!

Here are the answers to what has held Humanity back from achieving its ultimate goals and unlocking the true power of the Spirit and the highest state of Knowing and Being.

Carefully selected by Mardukite Publications Officer, James Thomas, this collection of eighteen critical articles, lecture transcripts and reference chapters by Joshua Free, is sure to be not only a treasured part of your personal collection, but this newly revised collector's edition hardcover is also the perfect introduction to the *Pathway* for friends & loved ones.

Drawn from nearly half-a-million words comprising the complete body of Master Grade Systemology literature developed by Joshua Free, now is the time to shine clear light on your own path as you realize...

...The Way Into The Future

TABLET OF CONTENTS

Titles in this Pathway-to-Self-Honesty Series:

Systemology: The Original Thesis

The Power of Zu

The Tablets of Destiny

Crystal Clear

Series abridged pocket anthology available as:

The Way Into the Future

Series also available in a complete anthology:

The Systemology Handbook

Gateways-to-Infinity Advanced Series Titles:

Metahuman Destinations

Imaginomicon

∞

PUBLISHER'S NOTE

"The Self does not actualize Awareness
past a point not understood."
—*Tablets of Destiny*

While preparing this book for publication, the editor and publisher have made every effort to present the material in a straightforward manner—using clear, easy to read and understand language.

Wherever a word that is defined in the glossary first appears in the main text, it will be **bold**.

This edition excerpts text from several titles. It is expected that a *Seeker* will work through this material multiple times to achieve optimum results. A clear understanding of this material is critical for achieving actual realizations and personal benefit from applying philosophies of *Mardukite Zuism* and *NexGen Systemology* spiritual technology.

The *Seeker* should be especially certain not to simply "read through" this book without attaining proper comprehension as "knowledge." Even when the information continues to be "interesting"—if at any point you find yourself feeling lost or confused while reading, trace your steps back. Return to the point of misunderstanding and go through it again.

Take nothing within this book on faith.
Apply the information directly to your life.
Decide for yourself.

∞

EDITOR'S PREFACE TO THE PREMIERE HARDCOVER COLLECTOR'S EDITION — "ONWARD AND UPWARD" —

When my long time friend and mentor—*Joshua Free*—came to me last year inquiring if I'd like to help with a new project, instantaneously I answered, "*Of course, yes!*" It had been a few years since I'd last been able to intensely assist with the "behind-the-scenes" side of things; and I must admit, I began feeling a bit like what I'd imagine King Arthur would have felt like, as a young adult, after he experienced time away from Merlyn, only to have him suddenly reappear again with new adventures and teachings in store!

Once initial excitement settled—and once I had a better idea of what this project would be—it was time to get down to work. The goal was clear enough: essentially, to craft a basic book—an introductory "*Best-Of*" sampler—drawn from existing Grade-III Mardukite Systemology material. This sounded all fine and good initially, but once the first day of note taking and editing began, that anxious feeling swept over. How could one take something as important and "next level" as *Systemology* and whittle it down to it's most "important" and introductory parts? It *all* seemed important to me; because it is. This was clearly not going to be a quick reordering of a few chapters. I did the only thing I thought right to do. I started back at the beginning of the Systemology materials, and worked my way up through them again, taking notes and experimenting with different chapter orders as I went. No skimming; no skipping around.

It actually took longer than I had initially thought, but I kept *Joshua* in the loop as I went—making certain to give the work the full respect and time it deserved, in order to develop the most optimal final product. Finally, when everything felt totally cohesive, well ordered, and all around proper, I sent it off to Joshua. Once it had his final edits and stamp of approval, I felt incredibly confident about the presentation and couldn't wait to see a hard-copy and experience the results in person.

I communicate this about my hand in the creative process behind "*Way Into The Future: A Handbook For The New Human*" not to make it sound like a taxing chore—as it most certainly was not; quite the opposite—but to reinforce just how monumentally important *Mardukite Systemology* is to those actively studying it, and applying it, to their current existence. Those of you who know, *know*. Those of you who don't yet know, will most undoubtedly understand soon. It was no easy task to decide what *was* and *was not* going to make the cut for this book, which leads me to make my main point:—

> What our *Systemology Society* has been able to achieve thus far has been astounding. There is *nothing* else like *Systemology* out there; and if you doubt that, just give it a try. "Apply the acid test yourself," as Joshua says.

Our goal here is to present a useful book to both newcomers and those familiar with Systemology alike. For those of you returning yet again, we hope this book serves you as an invaluable reference and guide wherever you may be in life. For those just starting upon the *Pathway*, or who may even just carry a slight interest in this, *welcome!* We expect this book to provide you with a solid optimal "launch point" for a better life. While it is true, this collection is only a tip of the iceberg, once you discover what our *Systemology* is, what it can do for you, and what it means for each and every one of us, I'm sure you'll immediately want to dive right into past (and future) work because... well, *who wouldn't?*

I won't suspend you in an excessively lengthy forward. But, I'd like you to know that great care has been taken in constructing this present tome, because *the work* is deserving of that; and *You* are deserving of that. So, onwards and upwards we go, friends!

~ James Thomas
May 19, 2021

THE WAY INTO THE

FUTURE

A HANDBOOK FOR THE NEW HUMAN

— MARDUKITE ZUISM — A BRIEF INTRODUCTION*

According to the most ancient historical records written at the birth of our modern civilization...

432,000 years ago, a small population of advanced beings—called the ANUNNAKI—began developing the planet Earth for their purposes. These elite Self-Actualized spiritual beings resided on Earth in physical bodies, but found their forms inadequate for the physical labors required. Enter: the "Human Condition." Ancient "cuneiform" tablet writings from Sumerians and Babylonians of Mesopotamia are clear regarding the original creation and systematic programming of Humanity.

> CUNEIFORM is the oldest known writing system used by scribes of ancient Babylon to record their wisdom and the history of humanity on clay tablets.

"Cuneiform" is named for its style of wedge-shaped script formed by a reed pen called a "stylus." Rather than an alphabet of letters, cuneiform writing is a system of "signs" representing "things" and "ideas." These may even be combined to represent even more complex "signs."

Many concepts adopted for modern "Mardukite Zuism" and its "Systemology" are derived from cuneiform tablets.

The ANUNNAKI introduced complex writing systems in order to program civilization and all parameters of Reality for the Human Condition. Legendary "Tablets of Destiny" (Divine Truth, supreme knowledge and cosmic power of the "gods") were first introduced to Humanity in the Babylonian narrative known best as the "Epic of Creation.

---

* "*Mardukite Zuism: A Brief Introduction*" Revised Version 2.0.

THE ARCANE TABLETS.

Ancient Babylonians used the *Tablets of Destiny & Creation Epic* to systematize all cosmic knowledge into a workable paradigm called "Mardukite Zuism"—a systemology received directly from the ANUNNAKI.

> PARADIGM : all-encompassing standard or religion used to view the world and communicate reality.
>
> SYSTEMOLOGY : applied philosophies (of *Mardukite Zuism*) combined with personal spiritual techniques and technology ("*Tech*") effectively demonstrating systematic principles of a "paradigm."

THE SYSTEMOLOGY OF LIFE, UNIVERSES & EVERYTHING.

The *Arcane Tablets* describe the division of the ALL by the LAW, outside of which is but INFINITY. The *Epic of Creation* describes these activities as "mythology." The "Standard Model of Systemology" that is applied to *Mardukite Zuism* uses the same information to demonstrate...

> that ALL ("AN-KI") envelops both:
> the Spiritual Existences ("AN")
> and the Physical Existences ("KI")
> divided by Cosmic Law and
> connected by Life-Awareness ("ZU")
> and beyond which is only the Abyss,
> an Infinity of Nothingness ("ABZU")

MARDUKITE ZUISM DEFINITIONS FOR STANDARD MODEL OF SYSTEMOLOGY.

> ABZU = the Abyss; Infinity; Infinity of Nothingness; that which extends, is exterior to and beyond of, all spiritual and physical existence.

ANKI : the ALL; All Existences; Everything that is AN and KI; Everything that is conceivable; represented by the "Standard Model of Systemology."

AN : the "Spiritual Universe" or "Heavenly Zone" comprised of spiritual energy-matter, in the direction of Infinity—the "Alpha" existence independent of, and superior to, the physical, *beta* or KI.

KI : the "Physical Universe" or "Earthly Zone" comprised of physical energy-matter in action across physical Space and observed as Time in the direction of Physical Continuity—"beta" existence condensed from, and subordinate to, the spiritual, *Alpha* or AN.

ZU L "to know"; "knowingness"; "Awareness" or "consciousness"; spiritual energy-matter of AN observed as "Lifeforce" in KI; "Spiritual Life Energy"; the actual personal spiritual beingness or "Awareness" of Self as the Alpha-Spirit which extends along a "line" from the Spiritual (AN) to the Physical (KI).

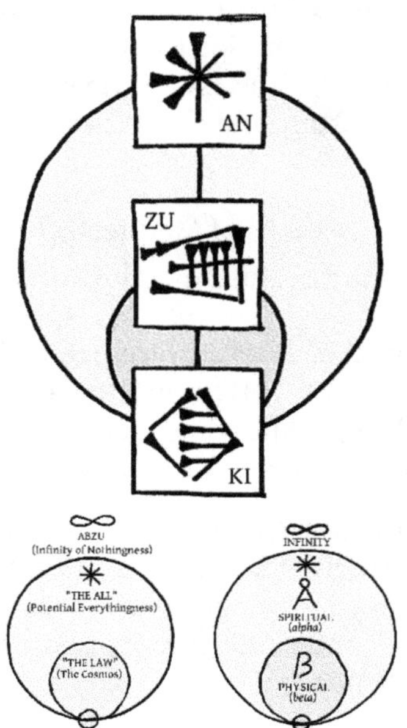

THE TABLETS OF DESTINY & BABYLONIAN CREATION EPIC.

Seven cuneiform tablets compose the ancient Babylonian Epic of Creation, named the Enuma Eliš by scholars after its opening lines. These seven tablets are the basis for what later traditions refer to as the "*Seven Days of Creation.*" The *Epic of Creation* tablets describe development of all existences with a Divine artistic perfection. The *Enuma Eliš* is the core example of religious literature from Babylon, which served as the basis for ancient "*Mardukite Zuism*"—the first true systematized religion in history.

> The Absolute *behind* and *back of* ALL Existence is referred to on the *Tablets of Destiny* as the INFINITY OF NOTHINGNESS; a constant static latent unmanifest potentiality of ALL and Everythingness.

The LAW—Cosmic Law—is defined as the Cosmic Dragon—TIAMAT—on "*Epic of Creation*" Tablets. She is the First Cause or movement across a "Sea of Infinity." Later, the LAW becomes a division between Spiritual Existence (AN) and any Physical Universe (KI). The LAW—*Tiamat*—permeating ALL, uses the *Tablets of Destiny* and then fixes the systems of finite potential:

The Systems of Manifestation—
Substance, Motion and Awareness.

> "Before 'Heaven' or 'Earth' were named," a formation and interaction of active existences—"substances" and "bodies" and "Life" and "gods"—creates turbulence and waves of action through space.
>
> The governing system of Cosmic Law—*Tiamat*—responds accordingly. She fixes the *Tablets of Destiny* to her "deputy"—a messenger wave action of the LAW named "*Kingu*" and sends him rippling out to "meet" the *Anunnaki* "gods."

The *Anunnaki Assembly* of "gods" prepare to battle The LAW. When none among them comes forth to engage, the *Anunnaki* "god" MARDUK volunteers as hero to confront *Kingu* and *Tiamat*—but with a condition that the *Anunnaki Assembly* recognize him as "Chief of the Gods" upon his success.

When *Marduk* approaches *Tiamat* (LAW) directly, he is flanked by *Kingu* and the "army of Ancient Ones." *Marduk* relinquishes the *Tablets of Destiny* from *Kingu*. With the *Tablets of Destiny*, *Marduk* successfully conquers the true understanding of "Cosmic Law" and thereby conquers *Tiamat*.

THE TABLETS OF DESTINY & SELF-HONESTY.

Marduk uses the Tablets of Destiny to discover "Self-Honesty" and Divine Knowledge governing "Cosmic Ordering"—systems dividing the "Spiritual Universe" (AN) from a "Physical Universe" (KI).

> The two Universe types are connected only by a stream of Spiritual Awareness (*Lifeforce*) that Sumerians called ZU.

Wisdom of the Arcane Tablets is later passed down to and concealed by an ancient esoteric secret society in Babylon: the Scribe-Magicians, High Priests and Priestesses of *Mardukite Zuism*.

Self-Honestyis a term describing an original "Alpha" state of clear knowingness and Self-directed beingness."Self-Honesty" is the most basic and true expression of Self as "I-AM"—free of artificial attachments; reactive-response conditioning; and imposed or enforced programming as Reality for the Human Condition. Spiritual development in modern *Mardukite Zuism* is referred to as the "Pathway to Self-Honesty" and the "Gateway to Infinity." It is modeled directly from the Ancient Mystery Tradition as observed at the original Temples of Babylon.

KEYS TO THE GATEWAY

> "I will take my Blood—and with Bone—I will fashion a Race of Humans to keep Watch of the Gate. And from the Blood of Kingu I will create another Race of Humans to inhabit the Earth in service to the Gods—so shrines to the Anunnaki may be built and the temples filled. I will bind the Elder Gods to the Watchtowers; let them keep watch over the Gate of Abzu and the Gate of Tiamat and Gate of Kingu—and with a Key that shall be ever hidden, known to none, except only to my Mardukites."
>
> — MARDUK, *Enuma Eliš, Creation Tablet VI.*

THE ANUNNAKI LADDER OF LIGHTS & BABYLONIAN GATEWAYS TO INFINITY.

ZIGGURAT TEMPLES in Babylonia—and throughout Mesopotamia—served to remind populations of the "bond" or ZU connecting "Heaven" and "Earth." Seven-stepped "levels" of the physical *Ziggurat Temples* of Babylonia—and seven corresponding Gates—represent spiritual levels of actualized Awareness; states of Self-purification (or "spiritual defragmentation") as they ascend in the direction of AN toward Infinity of Supreme Beingness—the Pathway of Self-Honesty—in imitation of the footsteps of the gods during their descent through the "spheres" or "Gates."

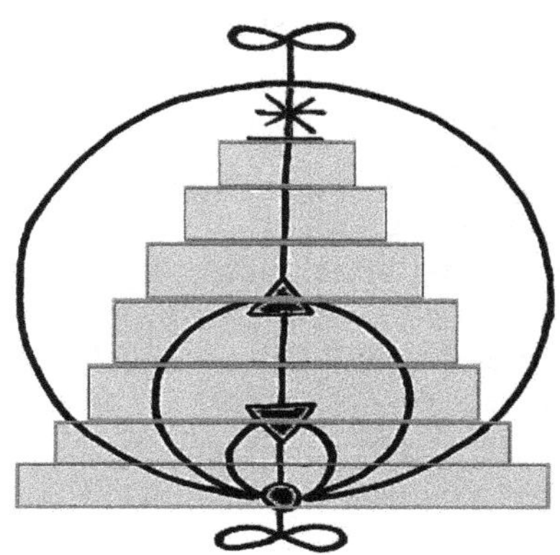

COSMOLOGY AND METAPHYSICS.

All Things in the Physical Universe are in motion—wave motions of "energy and matter in space measured as-and-across time." Continuity of the Physical Universe (KI) is divided by LAW and encompassed by the ALL (ANKI). The direction of AN extends toward ABZU, an Infinity of Nothingness beyond effective existence.

> The Alpha Self or Alpha Spirit is the true source—the "spiritual cause" of "physical effects." It engages Self-determined WILL from its "spiritual" Alpha existence as an Actualized Awareness impinging on "physical" Beta existence and experienced as "Life."

USING ANCIENT WISDOM TO UNLOCK HUMAN POTENTIAL.

Communication of clear wisdom and true knowledge from Arcane Tablets is distorted as it passes through time and geography, diverse languages and authoritarian cultures using the "Power" to program the masses and fragment the Human Condition away from Self-Honesty.

> Use of this ancient wisdom reveals the Keys to "Cosmic Ordering"—applying the highest understanding of "cause-and-effect" sequences to all action in the Physical Universe, and to all *Self-directed* applications of WILL-Intention and Effort.

MARDUKITE ZUISM, SYSTEMOLOGY & SPIRITUALITY.

The Spiritual Universe (AN)—of metaphysical or spiritual energy and metaphysical or spiritual matter is not dependent on the Physical Universe (KI) to exist; the two are existentially independent of each other, maintaining a single channel, conduit or connection, which is Alpha Spirit "Awareness" as Spiritual Life or ZU.

The Alpha Spirit engages a ZU-line, a spiritual lifeline of ZU energy to a genetic vehicle or organic body to experience physical beta existence.

MARDUKITE ZUISM DEFINITIONS FOR METAHUMAN SYSTEMOLOGY.

ALPHA SPIRIT : a Spiritual *life-form*; the True Self or "I-AM"; a unit of *Awareness;* a *Spiritual Beingness* that controls a physical body or "genetic vehicle" using a Lifeline or continuum of spiritual "ZU" energy.

ASCENSION : actualized Awareness elevated to (AN) spiritual existence that is exterior to beta-existence; the ability to *Self-direct* from *Spirit* as *Self* in existence independent of any "body."

BETA-EXISTENCE : manifestation of a Physical Universe (KI); conditions of energy-matter manifested in a state of condensed existence matching frequencies specific to space in the Physical Universe.

FRAGMENTATION : breaking apart; scattering the pieces; fractioning wholeness; fracture of holism; discontinuity; a separation of totality; anything outside or apart from original clarity (or *Self-Honesty*).

GENETIC VEHICLE : Physical *life-form*; physical (*beta*) body controlled by an Alpha Spirit using a continuous Lifeline of ZU energy; an organic catalyst for a Spirit to operate causes and observe effects (in *beta*).

HUMAN CONDITION : a standard issue default programmed state of Human experience; receptacle for Alpha Spirit Awareness that is generally accepted to be the extent of its potential identity (*Beingness*).

ZU-LINE : Spiritual Life-Energy (ZU) continuum; an energetic channel or Identity-Continuum connecting Alpha Spirit Awareness from Infinity-to-Infinity including the full Physical or *beta* range of existence.

THE HIGHEST FORM OF TRUE DIVINE WORSHIP.

The true Destiny of Humanity is to achieve spiritual Self-Actualization; the reunion of Self with the Infinite.

Attaining Self-Honesty in this Life is the most important step a person can take toward achieving their highest ideals, goals and realizations as a Spiritual Being.

The Highest form of "True Worship" begins with the Spirit —the true Self—and all external practices, rituals, ceremonies and historical examples are but outer reflections of this ideal. The Highest form of "Sin" is against the Spirit—against the Self—and its ability to maintain Self-Honesty.

There are modes of thought, action and Self-direction of effort that will contribute toward Ascension; and modes that lead away from that.

Beta experiences of "Sin"—pain, fear, guilt, anger—are all related to personal fragmentation; and emotional turbulence from all of these may be released—and intention energy redirected—because:

We all co-create the reality we experience in this lifetime!

SPHERES OF EXISTENCE AND INFLUENCE & A UTILITARIAN SYSTEMOLOGY OF ETHICS.

The prime directive of all beta existence is: *to exist*. The continuation of existence is the purpose behind all existence. Between realization of Self and Infinity, there are many spheres of existence that we may influence.

All of the spheres are interconnected. There is nothing in existence that is in absolute exclusion to all existence. Each sphere of existence supports subsequent existences and assists reaches toward higher spheres of influence.

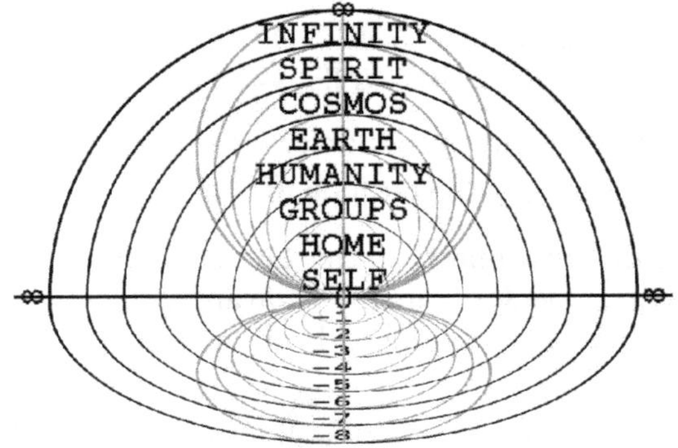

The greatest good contributes to the greatest continuation of optimum existence and survival for the greatest sphere of inclusion. Degrees of rightness and wrongness are determined by Cosmic Law and are reflected in the quality and continuation of optimal existence at the highest sphere of existence. Individual happiness is attained via the channel to the highest sphere. Unhappiness is a result of "selfishness," lack of "Spiritual Self-Actualization" and/or reach of "Actualized Awareness" beyond *Self* as identified to a *body*.

ZU : MARDUKITE ZUISM & MODERN ZUIST RELIGION.

History demonstrates how dangerous, troublesome and easily misused the concept of "RELGION" is; so, for purposes of incorporating *Mardukite Zuism* and its *Systemology* as a contemporary standard, the idea is treated here as defined.

> RELIGION : a concise spiritual paradigm, fixed set of beliefs and practices, regarding Divinity, Infinite Beingness—or else "God."

—*Mardukite Zuism* operates under a premise of very specific beliefs and "systemology" of "applied spiritual technology."

—*Mardukite Zuist Religious Doctrine* fundamentally relays the previously described "Highest forms" of Worship, Cosmic Law, and Ethics.

Mardukite Zuist Spiritual Doctrines and its *Systemology* successfully meet modern "religious" criteria for:

a) A Description of Cosmic Creation;
b) Belief in a Supreme Infinite Being;
c) Ethics Leading to Human Ascension;
d) Ethics of Conduct Toward all Life and Existence;
e) Immortality of the Human Spirit;
f) A Published Library of Religious Literature;
g) Traditions of Practice and Application; and
h) A Spiritual Advisement Methodology.

GOALS & IDEALS OF MARDUKITE ZUISM.

The word "ZU" meant "knowing" in original Sumerian cuneiform script. Goals and ideals of Zuism reflect this. *Mardukite Zuism & Systemology* seeks to assist an individual in reclaiming a total realization of the True Self or "I-AM" knowingly as the Immortal Alpha Spirit, in line with a most ancient directive: to "Know Thyself."

In view of the fact that all modern humans are subjected to technologies depriving them of their freedoms to *be*, *think*, *know* and pursue truth: goals and ideals of *Mardukite Zuism & Systemology* are to effectively repair abilities and elevate certainty of an Individual to increase and direct "Actualized Awareness" toward Higher Gateways of Spiritual Ascension.

INFINITY, "GOD" & SUPREME BEINGNESS

Spiritual Philosophy of *Mardukite Zuism* is systematized by a Standard Model of Systemology. It demonstrates Absolute Supreme Beingness associated with the Highest realization of "God" as INFINITY. No thing is Higher or Absolute than the *Infinity of Nothingness*—and reducing Supreme Beingness to any finite personality or character trait is to limit and defile what is herewith represented, but with lesser "words" and mundane sentiments or semantics.

The Highest Name of God cannot be conceived
—hence our symbolic use of the Infinity Sign:

...or Sumerian cuneiform word-sign: "ABZU"—
"The Infinite Nothingness and Source of All ZU."

—The Spiritual Universe (AN) is *All-as-One* because it exists as an infinite singularity or stasis: infinite potential with no gradient or observed motion; which is its own continuity.

—The Physical Universe (KI) is *All-as-One* because it is in continuous motion, with all manifest parts working systematically as the condensed solid continuity of beta-existence.

—A "spiritual continuum" or "conduit channel" of ZU (or a "*Zu-line*") from a Spiritual Universe (AN)—links our Awareness levels of "I-AM," "True Self" or Spirit ("Alpha Spirit") with varying potential "Point-of-View" and degrees of motion experienced in the Physical Universe.

—The Alpha Spirit or "Soul" is the true Awareness, "I" or "Self" connected to the operation and control of the physical body.

BASIC CONCEPT OF THE HUMAN SPIRIT.

The true Self is the "I" or "I-AM" or "Spirit"
regardless of its *perceived* position in spaces,
Point-of-View, degree or level of Awareness.
Spirit remains at its original fixed true point.

Whatever "spiritual energy-matter" (*if any*) that may compose the Alpha Spirit or makeup of "soul"—it must occupy this "other space" with its spiritual existence and then project its Awareness and Will onto the Physical Universe (KI) in order to experience the *Game* we call "*Life.*"

This "*Spiritual Life Energy*" or *Awareness* of a *Spiritual Being* is treated as a "Lifeforce" and "Consciousness" and goes by many names throughout the history of language, mysticism and spirituality—but we find the idea first treated as ZU on cuneiform tablets of Mesopotamia.

> On an Identity-lifeline or continuum of ZU energy, an Alpha Spirits is operating from a Spiritual Universe to experience in *beta-existence*. We refer to this concept as the "*ZU-line*" on the Standard Model of Systemology to illustrate the projected Awareness from Spirit (as an epicenter or fixed point) to any other *Point-of-view* (POV) anywhere in existence.

ZU is the name given to the spiritual beingness or essence of all Life in existence—and Self is a concentrated center or focal point that projects Awareness on a ZU-continuum or Zu-line toward a point of artificial Identity separate from Self.

The True Self of an Individual Human is a "spiritual universe cause" of "physical universe effects"—engaging as an immortal Alpha Spirit with a Self-determined Will actualized as an Awareness along a ZU-continuum (or "*Zu-line*"), extending from Infinity-to-Infinity, through every possible frequency and vibration along the total spectrum of physical and metaphysical existence.

THE SYSTEMOLOGY OF SPIRITUAL ADVISEMENT COUNSELING PRACTICES FOR MARDUKITE ZUISM

The Mardukite Chamberlains, an underground research organization established in 2009, dedicated itself to recovery and consolidation of relevant historical, scriptural & ritual records of ancient Mardukite Babylon in Mesopotamia, following up the founding of Mardukite Ministries (Mardukite Zuism) by Joshua Free the previous year, in 2008.

By 2011, a Mardukite Alumni faction (International Systemology Society) began research and development into new methods of:

> applying ancient wisdom as a futurist spiritual technology that effectively awakens, unlocks and fully actualizes spiritual potential of the Human Condition.

A systematic and logical approach to spirituality is visibly demonstrable on the Standard Model of Systemology, where ZU-line frequencies are represented at various degrees:

- "zero-point" body death;
- cellular life and sensory perceptions of a genetic body;
- bio-chemicals induced by emotion;
- thoughts and intention transmitted between our Alpha Spirit and the "genetic vehicle"—
- all the way "up" the scale to a perfected clarity of Self-Actualized Awareness of I-AM as our true "Alpha" state, just below Infinity and Absolute Beingness.

Full potential of ZU in is only altered from its natural state as a result of personal fragmentation of the Human Condition. This may be restored by systematic spiritual practices.

The *Pathway to Self-Honesty* is a personal journey and spiritual adventure marked by progressive clearing of personal energy channels fragmented by emotional imprinting and programming-data accumulated from "experiences" in the environment—the "debris" that fragments the total actualized experience of Self in Awareness as the Alpha Spirit.

The first and most important step—Before an individual can actualize potentials of the Spirit as Self, they must fully realize:

> The *I-AM Self* and the *Alpha Spirit* are One and the same. This state of Knowingness is a primary intention of basic spiritual practices of Mardukite Zuism & Systemology.

Mardukite Zuism materials, *Systemology* books and advanced training courses are available to Mardukite Ministers seeking qualification as specialized Clergy, Priests, Priestess, and Professional Pilots of systematic processing.

THE CREED OF MARDUKITE ZUISM. PRINCIPLES OF BELIEF.*

1.) We believe in an Absolute Being, which is Infinite —(the ABZU)—the All-as-One encompassing Source of all Being, Knowing and Awareness to all Alpha/Spiritual (AN) and Beta/Physical (KI) states of existence.

2.) We believe in a spiritual energy of all Life and Awareness (ZU) in the physical universe that is an effect of a spiritual cause; a Spirit that is cause. This Spirit—in its Alpha state—is the True Self "I-AM" Individual Identity that many have called the "soul."

3.) We believe that the Human Condition is a genetic vehicle used by a spiritual source (AN) to experience the Finite as physical existence (KI)—that we are Awareness (ZU) projected onto a genetic vehicle—and that while the vehicle/body may perish to physical entropy, the "Alpha Spirit" remains immortal and Self-directed to the extent of its own Actualized Awareness.

4.) We believe that the highest form of worship and spirituality is the actualization and advancement of our "Self" as Spirit in Self-Honesty—and that Self-Honesty is the I-AM Alpha state of Being and Knowing, which is realizable in this lifetime.

5.) We believe that the purpose of all existence is: to exist—and that the prime directive of all spiritual Life is: continued existence of spiritual Life and co-creation of habitable Reality. "Good" and "Moral" actions are evaluated to the extent of this end.

6A.) We believe that no Life exists in exclusion to all other Life—and that the conditions of a habitable

* First drafted in 2019 by Joshua Free with Kyra Kaos.

Reality extending from Self include: Home; Community; All Humanity; All Life on Earth; All Life in the Universe; All Spiritual Life; and the Infinite.

6B.) We believe in a continued evolution of Alpha Spirit awareness developed beyond one physical life, and that a Spirit experiences many.

7A.) We believe Mardukite Zuism is: a 21st Century AD synthesis of the 21st Century BC wisdom collected on cuneiform tablets and experienced in ancient Mesopotamia, esp. Babylon.

7B.) This cuneiform library includes details concerning: beings called the Anunnaki; ordering of the Cosmos; creation of Humanity; and an entire legacy of systematized traditions.

8.) We believe in the continuation of, and proper communication of, the legacy of true Human history —and the ability of every Human to realize that they are a Free Spirit in a Free Zone of Self-Determinism: No "evils" can affect intentions if an individual is spiritually Self-Actualized in Self-Honesty.

SIFTING THE SANDS OF TIME TO RECOVER WISDOM FROM THE CLAY: THE EVOLUTION OF OUR UNDERSTANDING

"*Your command shall be effective,*" says *Tiamat*—the *First Cause* —to *Kingu*, her **vizier** and cosmic messenger, as she transfers possession of the *Tablets of Destiny,* affirming: "*Whatsoever you will—it shall be established.*"

Here we open by paraphrasing the very sentiment applied to the "origins of Creation" as provided on the very first tablet of the **Babylonian "cosmology"** series. This is where our premiere **knowledge** of the *Tablets of Destiny* shows its face in perhaps the most **paramount** foundation text of the ancient Mardukite "**paradigm**"—the *Enuma Eliš*, or *Epic of Creation** of Babylon.

> ***paradigm*** : "an all-**encompassing** *standard* by which to view the world and *communicate* Reality; a **standard model** of reality-systems used by the Mind to filter, interpret and organize experience of Reality."

More "Mardukite ink" has been spilled regarding the *Enuma Eliš* than any other **cuneiform** tablet cycle. So, it might seem, at first glance, that there would be no *new* data to glean for our purposes. However, we have never provided a treatment of this cornerstone from the **degree** of ***Awareness*** attainable at our current **level** of **understanding**—Mardukite Systemology (*Grade-III*)—and certainly never before demonstrated publicly in connection to the elusive "*Tablets of Destiny,*" which appear throughout our most ancient texts as the definitive key to **commanding** true authority as *Self* in the physical universe.

* The full text of the "Epic of Creation" appears in *The Tablets of Destiny (Appendix)*—as excerpted from "Tablet-N" in *The Complete Anunnaki Bible* edited by Joshua Free; also reprinted for Mardukite Zuism in *Anunnaki Bible: New Standard Zuist Edition* and *Complete Book of Marduk by Nabu.*

For nearly a decade these matters remained privately in the domain of an advanced division of the "*Mardukite Research Organization*" known from its brief public references as the "*NexGen Systemological Society*" governing the new "*Mardukite Academy of Systemology.*" This faction has operated in the **esoteric** underground since 2011, developing a direct extension of the "Mardukite Core"§ to support research and discovery of continuing work, as it applies to the present state of the **"Human Condition"** and its imminent future.

At our "first level of understanding," the *Enuma Eliš* is a treatise regarding "magical practices" in ancient Babylon, contributing to the "**systematized** religion" distributed among the common **Mesopotamian** population. There are no shortage of rites and workable **methodologies** derivable at this level in which to occupy the civic mind and social awareness of humanity (at a physio-emotional degree of ***Awareness***). In fact, this is what has been going on for some time in **Western** civilization—at least 4,000 years—since the perfected Babylonian **codification** of Human systems. Even the data that appears fairly concrete within the confines of this "physical" level—including the vast **catalogs** of terminology and definitions provided by the physical sciences—may still fall under the category of "**superstition**" when treated at "higher" clearer degrees of *Awareness.*

Ancient efforts to successfully systematize the material world, using Babylonia as its **epicenter**, are attributed to the Anunnaki god "**Nabu**"—meaning "*speaker*" or "*prophet*"—who **heralded** a rise of the original ancient "Mardukite" *standard* in Babylon, in honor of his "father" *Marduk*, the central hero of the *Enuma Eliš*. This was accomplished by the establishment of a "priesthood"—a distinct learned portion of the general population—dispensing the "mysteries" from the "second level of understanding," us-

§ All "Grade-I" and "Grade-II" material pertaining to past systems of "magical," "mystical" or "religious" semantics, now available in Master Edition anthologies—*Necronomicon: The Complete Anunnaki Legacy*, *Merlyn's Complete Book of Druidism* and *The Great Magickal Arcanum.*

ing the "written word" as their medium—something incredibly revolutionary for its time. In doing so, the "*Mardukite paradigm*"—at an exclusively "intellectual **degree** of awareness"—became a global standard, perpetually influencing worldly systems of the Human Condition in every social **institution** imaginable: philosophy of **individualism**; management of family life; the structure of societal roles; and even world order. All of which is reflected by an intellectual treatment of wisdom from these proverbial "*Tablets of Destiny*."

> ***self-honesty*** : "the ***alpha*** state; clear and present total *Awareness* of-and-as *Self*, in its most basic and true proactive expression of itself as *Spirit* or *I-AM*—free of artificial attachments, perceptive filters and other emotionally-reactive or mentally-conditioned programming imposed on the human condition by the systematized physical world."

The "third level of understanding" is the highest degree—in total ***Self-Honest*** clarity of *Awareness* as *Self*—directly demonstrable from the "*Tablets of Destiny*." This incredibly superior level of **realization** is often **misappropriated** simply as "spiritual" in former philosophical and religious outlines throughout history—but in spite of vocabulary they may use, most philosophical and spiritual paradigms are still only treated, at best, from the "second level of understanding," as comprehended purely from an intellectual level by the "most educated" of those institutions. These folk tend to pride themselves on *their superior* scope of **discernment** regarding that particular vocabulary (and "**semantic**-set") within the realm or community that they operate. Very little of such arcane lore is information that *actually* and *observably* assists the **individual** or *Self* in achieving any higher levels of understanding—the purpose of which would be to advance an individual toward the point of "*Self-Honesty!*"

Most organizations—operating outside the scope of *Self-Honesty*—either lack the ability (*or desire*) to **evaluate** (*or el-*

evate) their "congregations" or "students" to such a caliber of ***Self-actualization*** and ***Self-determinism***. Many of these, which do maintain a ***responsibility*** to assist humanity in this way, fear losing their own civic control and the social dependence emphasizing the "Institution" above all. This focus disrupts the natural order of *Life*, disregarding completely the fundamental **existence** of the spiritually evolving *Individual* as its primary goal. It is here onward that we begin to recognize a definitive distinction between common "**exoteric**" public presentations (and understanding) of universal information and that which is frequently deemed "**esoteric,**" meaning a higher understanding of—and behind of—the same, that few are actually aware of.

We are *not* putting forth the suggestion that what we have discovered—and present within the scope of *Mardukite Systemology*—is in any way the *only* method whereby a person may truly reach this elevated state, which we have simply chosen to call ***Self-Honesty***. There are surprisingly quite a few individuals throughout history that *have* achieved this—and many of the more recognizable examples are often described as "Ascended Masters" or "spiritual leaders," even becoming central icons for later evolving "faiths" and "traditions."

In nearly all of such antiquated instances, these points of achievement are accounted for by the determination of an individual's *own* unique ability and *not* as a reflection, product or result of some **systematized** tradition, philosophical institution or environment. This is a problem we are applying solutions to within the ***parameters*** of the current level of work.

> ***parameters*** : "a defined range of possible variables within a model, **spectrum** or **continuum**."

Everywhere we turn today, there is an abundance of alleged avenues of "mysticism" and methods professing "enlightenment"—and many of these are, at least in part, drawn from the same stream of knowledge descending from the "**Ancient Mystery School.**" But as we move further along the

timeline through the modern "New Age," we still find these esoteric treatments handled in ***fragmented*** *exclusion* within the same "first" and "second" orders of potential understanding, and no greater.

> ***fragmentation*** : "the *fractioning* of wholeness or the *fracture* of a **holistic** interconnected *alpha* state, favoring observational Awareness of perceived connectivity between parts; also *discontinuity*; separation of a totality into parts; in ***NexGen Systemology***, a person outside a state of '*Self-Honesty*' is said to be '*fragmented*'."

Even the few which seem to approach some version of "*Self-Honest clarity*" resulting from half-measure efforts of "***Crossing the Abyss***" within their own paradigm often fall by the wayside. Even an adept institution generally might carry an ability to bring their students right up to the *Gate to the Abyss*—but those few which pass through still carrying the attachments and weights of a broken paradigm, are capsized from the Boat—left to sink or swim amidst a Sea of Infinity. And *that* is, at best, where previous structured implementations of the ancient wisdom from the "*Tablets of Destiny*" have led ***Seekers*** prior to our recent efforts.

Our presentation given in the volume titled "*Tablets of Destiny: Using Ancient Wisdom to Unlock Human Potential*" is the first time that "***NexGen Systemology***" has crossed paths directly with the "Mardukite paradigm" in public for the current era. This begins a new cycle of "*Mardukite Systemology*" material that emphasizes a *demonstration of ancient wisdom in present* ***time*** *for the future.* To accomplish this—in *Self-Honesty*—and to make it accessible to anyone, we are introducing the foundation principles—most appropriately—within the context of the "*Tablets of Destiny.*" We are, for the first time, treating this wisdom from the collected **holistic** understanding gained from the *first three* **tiers**—or *Gates*—of understanding, as represented by the ***ziggurat*** of Babylon. There is no great secret behind this part—we are taking our (I) *physical* understanding, transferring it to (II) *intellectual* wisdom philosophies, and finally, (III) *spiritual* applications with results that promote advancement and incorporation of the true *Self* as *Spirit* in *Self-Honesty* into our everyday *Life*.

It is my privilege to present this revolutionary new breakthrough to all ***Seekers*** for the first time—and usher in a new standard by which to chart the next spiritual evolution of humanity into the 2020's and beyond.

DECIPHERING SECRETS OF EXISTENCE FROM THE "TABLETS OF DESTINY"

If we examine this wide body of **allegorical** lore in its entirety—which we will hereafter simplify with a reference to "*Arcane Tablets*" or "*Tablets of Destiny*"—then we are left to **extrapolate** a great many of the definitive "truths" for ourselves in relation to other data that we find consistent in guiding us effectively toward a higher level of **understanding** and practical application. We must account for the distortions of language across time, which we may accomplish by applying intensive experimental research methods to any discoveries—but we may do so only within the observable parameters of the **Cosmos** and **Cosmic Law** which governs energy and matter across the **space** and **time** of the Physical Universe. We must account for the distortions in present time language, which we may overcome by giving clear **dynamic** definitions of our use of terminology along the way—as repeatedly demonstrated in previous lesson-units. A true **communication** of the "fundamentals" at this level of understanding is only accomplished by overcoming any barriers in language—to be certain we are definitive in our meaning of ***A-for-A***. Otherwise, this information runs the risk of fading into the background of ***Awareness*** as "just more words."

The "*Arcane Tablets*" are clear in their presentation of the Cosmos and Cosmic Order of the Chaotic motion **enacted** in the Physical Universe—and all *things* in the Physical Universe are indeed in motion, which is why they **exist**. The Physical Universe also carries the distinction of being defined by *things* **relative** to other *things*. And all *things* are *wave* motions—as energy and matter—in **space** measured across **time**. Which is what a "wave" is. Most understand this best in relation to distance traveled in a vehicle—as "miles-*per*-hour" or "kilometers-*per*-hour" or what have you—which is always given a "space over time" or, if you prefer, "space divided by time." This is **localized** knowledge from the point of the Observer or *Self*—who is not moving, but is actually experiencing motion of the physical mechanics at work. This is why we often refer to these aspects as "**relative**" at such levels of understanding—therefore, we see, as the first ***Self-determined*** act by the **sentient** "***Alpha Spirit***" hero—in this case, "**Marduk**"—is to understand the Chaos of the Physical Universe and immediately apply efforts to Order it—and essentially, *create* with it.

> ***dynamic (systems)*** : "a principle or fixed system which demonstrates its *'variations'* in activity (or output) only in constant relation to variables or fluctuation of interrelated systems; a standard principle, function, process or system that exhibits *'variations'* and change simultaneously with all connected systems."

"Cosmological" or "cosmogenetic" origin epics—of which the *Enuma Eliš* is our most ancient and complete *Anunnaki* rendering on tablets used to systematize the Human Condition from a Babylonian epicenter—always, by definition, consist of **sentient** attempts to *Order* the *Chaos*. Creation, as we have been able to understand it, is not a true physical "creation" at all, but an *ordering*. "**Marduk**" is not, by any means, *creating* the energy and matter of the Physical Universe—he *is* applying his ***Will*** to be the "spiritual cause" of "physical effects" from a higher point of *Awareness* that is somehow outside or apart from the Physical Universe. This is clear with the perception of *Tiamat*—the *Law*—as suddenly "dualistic": separating a higher encompassing "Spiritual" state of existence from the Physical Universe.

To the extent that we have currently determined, the two Universes are independent of interaction from one another to exist, except by one *pathway*—and the instance of one singular expression—which is *Life*. As far as we know, the Spiritual Universe (of metaphysical energy and metaphysical matter) is not dependent on the Physical Universe (of physical energy and physical matter) to exist; nor, as we can easily observe, is the Physical Universe dependent on a Spir-

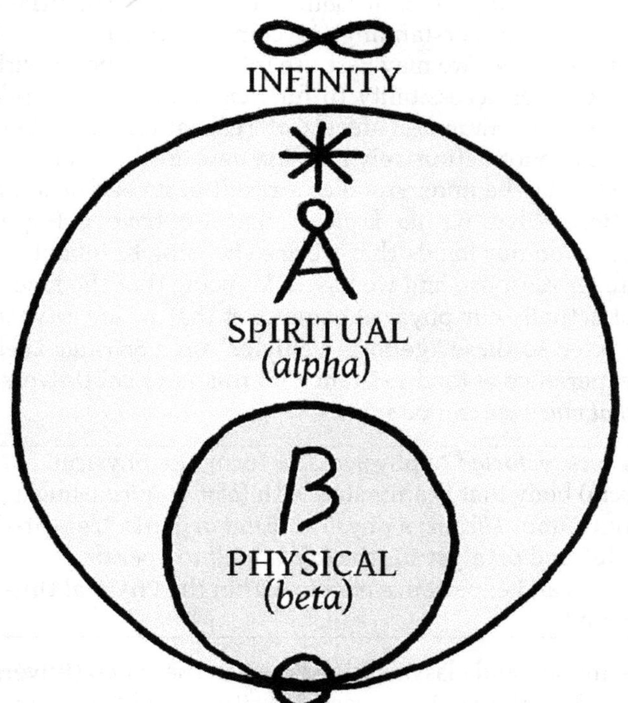
INFINITY
SPIRITUAL
(alpha)
PHYSICAL
(beta)

itual Universe to remain in its active motions—except when it comes to *Life* experienced within the Physical Universe. And we can visibly see that this Spiritual Universe has the ability to animate physical organisms with *Spiritual Energy* as *Life* to experience the Physical Universe.

Once we are in a state of **realization** about "*what*" is taking place, the "*whys*" behind the phenomenon of *Spiritual Life Energy* inhabiting *Physical Matter* seem inconsequential (at this level of understanding) in comparison to "*how*" this works and "*how*" we may best use information that *is* within our degree of accessibility to further us in greater understanding and *Awareness*—levels of realization at a plateau that we cannot definitively imagine now until we achieve it. The *why* may be understood as a result of its *Self-Honest* application. What we *do know* is that we have a Physical Universe on our hands that we are choosing to inhabit—for whatever reasons—and we have a knowing that the true *Self* is not actually our physical bodies, yet that *we are very much* connected to these "**genetic vehicles**" on a *Spiritual Lifeline* for experience *of* (and existence *in*) this Physical Universe—for *that much* we can be sure.

> ***genetic vehicle*** : "a physical *Life*-form; the physical (*beta*) body that is animated with (*alpha*) *Spirit* using a continuous *Lifeline*; a physical (*beta*) **organic "receptacle"** and **catalyst** for the (*alpha*) *Self* to operate causes and experience effects within the Physical Universe."

A distinction and classification between these two Universes is too often blurred in modern "spiritual" and "metaphysical" philosophies—and often too esoteric for many to easily decipher from the ancient sources, which was actually the intention of the "*Ancient Mystery School.*" Yet, to accomplish anything more than intellectual pleasure of **pilfering** obscure methodologies in search of confirmations to the already obscure conclusions **authoritatively** dictated by those with no real means of knowing the nature of the Spiritual Universe. Those folks quick to pat themselves on the back for rejecting **authoritarian** "religious dogma" of the Spiritual Universe (and its **causative** nature on the Physical Universe) are just as likely to **succumb** to another common trap, when the pendulum swings to the other extreme and we **systematize** the Physical Universe—including its unique interaction as *Life*—without any regard for the *Spirit*, of which conventional science has no better means of achieving an understanding of than with the ***Singularity*** it still seeks in its **logic equations**, because both are of the same *causal* "*Spiritual* ∞ *Infinity*" existing outside the boundaries of our *effective* "*Physical* ° ***Continuity***."

All **communication** of our Reality is conducted in relative terms—essentially from the perspective of the Physical Universe: Existence to the extent that we are **capable** of, or instructed in, reception, experience and understanding. This is relative also to the point of the **individual** Observer and the range of **faculties** at whatever **tier** of understanding and *Awareness* their perceptions are operating at. This is a natural part of **evaluating** our experience of Reality—for we are all here with the faculties of a *spiritual scientist*. Just as we see in physical terms of our *Awareness* for things—and the magnitude of definitions in our scope—the *Pathway* marking levels of *Awareness* between variable "degrees of **continuity**" in the Physical Universe (**"KI"** or "*beta*" state of existence) and "**static** infinity" governing the Spiritual Universe (**"AN"** or "*alpha*" state of existence) were once literally represented with ancient Babylonian temple infrastructures of ***Marduk*** and ***Nabu***—the ***ziggurats***—"stepped-pyramids" comprised of seven **tiers** connecting the Physical Universe with the "heavens."

The further up the levels—or "gates"—of the *ziggurat* one climbs, the greater the span of view achieved, and the "higher state of *Awareness*" accessible. It is progressive and cumulative. We are not losing a sense of previous levels of *Awareness*—though we may choose to no longer fixate on them, for to keep our balance we must be present and moving ahead. We are ***ascending***—and so from *this side*, we are not at first spreading our view so wide into the highest spiritual matters as to neglect the development of a strong foundation of understanding. It is for this reason that in our natural state of existence, we are always in the tendency toward the "higher" for our own physical survival and evolution of our physical existence in the Physical Universe ("**KI**") as **precedent** of our realizing or **actualizing** our spiritual infinity within the Physical Universe. *Life* that is not operating in this tendency is being *blocked*. And what's more, it is probably blocking or **inhibiting** other *Life*. We must assume that any *Life* operating against the **holistic** principles of its own physical and spiritual survival (which are relatively identical in the Physical Universe) is otherwise not in "good shape." They are applying efforts against their own survival—and that of others—and folk generally refer to these people as something synonymous with "unbalanced" or "fragmented."

Naturally, many among the ancient populations could not conceive of such *esoterica*—so they relied on the most physical **manifestations** to understand what they could not otherwise understand. And this is a tendency of "training our thought" that continues to be popular today—such as when we use metaphors to relay abstraction. But, those uninitiated to the "Ancient Mystery School" were only, at best, aware of the lowest levels of physical sensation and response-based reality experience programmed into the Human Condition. And again, not much has changed in this respect either regarding the general Human population. In fact, even today, we must continue to correct so many mistaken **associations** of the Spiritual Universe ("**AN**") with the "**space** *up there*."

The space encompassing the Earth planet is still *physical space*—and physical space reflects the "physical **continuity**" of the Physical Universe ("**KI**") which we represent with the symbol of a "circle" or "zero" (sometimes with a horizontal line through it)—also used in the sense of *degrees* of "**spectrum** on a continuum."

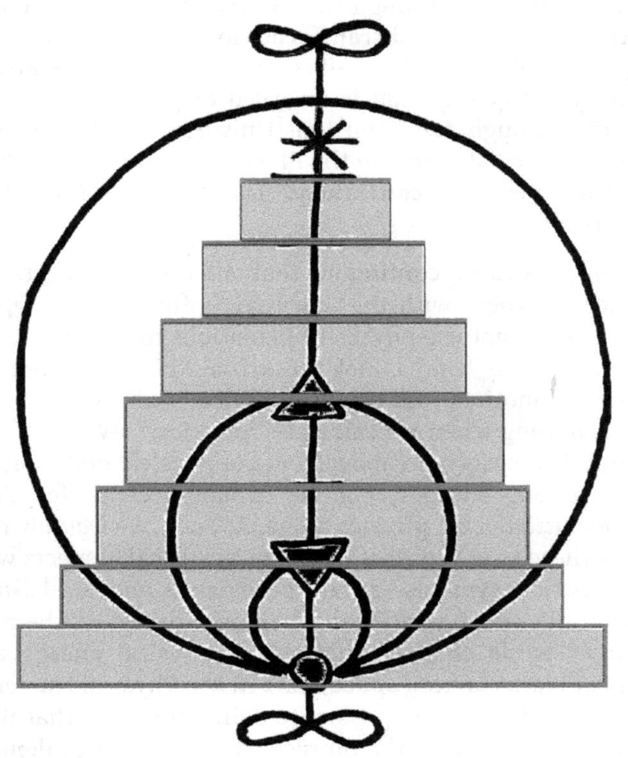

> ***continuum*** : "a continuous *whole*; observing all **gradients** on a *spectrum*; measuring quantitative variation with gradual transition on a spectrum without demonstrating discontinuity or separate parts."

Some esoteric schools have defined this continuum and its parameters regarding the Physical Universe as "*The Law*" or ***Cosmic Law***. Yet, although we find the Physical Universe as continuous motion and transformation—maybe even relatively **recursive** upon itself—it is not a true Infinite-**Static** or "Infinity"—a quality that is reserved only for the *Life* that projects through the "Spiritual Universe" relative to our ability to calculate for it in the Physical Universe. The Physical Universe is a ***continuity***. The Spiritual Dimension borders *Infinity*.

The only **band** or continuum that *All-as-One* connects the Physical "zeroes" with the Spiritual "infinities" is *Life*, for which we cannot use physical calculations to accurately describe, because "*Life*" is not the actual "physical" force of "physical" motion. And physical motion is all that what we are examining when we calculate "**physics**." We can fairly accurately measure the movements of physical bodies in relation to one another, but we cannot account for ***Self-determination*** using **physics** alone. As such, we *logically* represent these true "Spiritual" or "metaphysical" aspects with mathematical symbols—*zeroes* and *infinities* and *Greek letters* —that only seem irrational when we disregard them as "Source" while charting motions of physical energy and physical matter across **space-time** in the Physical Universe. No calculation exists in physics to define the *Spirit* that ***Wills*** an arm to move—only the physical (**kinetic**) energy demonstrated by the physical body during this action is measured.

We can demonstrate all manners of **semantic** logic to define how the body functions and this or that muscle in combination with electrical charges of the brain-center are carried out to accomplish the physical motion in **agreement** with Cosmic Law of the Physical Universe, but that is it. That is the extent of *knowingness* via **physiology**. And it is certainly valid to the extent of its truth in the Physical Universe. It makes **postulates** as to how actions and motions of the "genetic vehicle" carry it across the terrain, but it does not define the *driver*—and it never will. There is an equally *logical* reason for this—and we may extract it directly from the *Arcane Tablet* narrative of **Marduk.**

Marduk conquers Tiamat by first attaining the "*Tablets of Destiny*"—an understanding of *Cosmic Law*, the physical laws governing the Physical Universe—and then using them. He is *not* changing the Law. He is *not* spontaneously generating new solids from Spiritual Nothingness. Marduk is using the energy and matter of the Physical Universe and turning it back onto the Physical Universe *within* the parameters of Cosmic Law. He is the **causative *Will*** of action from a higher state, but he is not the physical force behind it. Those forces are already existent within the Physical Universe, and they have laws governing tendencies of their motion—which operate with or without our *agreement*. In fact, our ability to exist and evolve our form within the Physical Universe of these motions is entirely **conditional** on our "correctness" in evaluating our state of Reality *agreements* with the Physical Universe. Our degree of "incorrectness" seems to result in everything from pain to death.

An ***Alpha Spirit*** manifesting or projected from the Spiritual Universe chooses, for whatever reasons, to animate and operate a *Lifeform*. They may then thereafter, if somehow disturbed or fragmented out-of-**phase**, choose not to be in *agreement* with the Physical Universe. But unless their Reality is in a stronger state of agreements than Cosmic Law—which is, to us, an impossibility as far as we know, if still confining *Awareness* to the physical body—they will soon discover that they experience physical effects to their causes. This is not a "Divine" punishment; nor is it arbitrary. All effects of manifestation are according to parameters of the Cosmic Law of the Physical Universe. These are consequential to survival of anything within physical existence.

> ***alpha spirit*** : "a 'spiritual' *Life*-form; the 'true' *Self* or I-AM; the spiritual (*alpha*) *Self* that is animating the (*beta*) physical body or *'genetic vehicle'* using a continuous *Lifeline*; an individual spiritual (*alpha*) entity possessing no physical mass or measurable waveform (motion) in the Physical Universe as itself, so it animates the (*beta*) physical body or *'genetic vehicle'* as a **catalyst** to experience *Self*-determined causality in effect within the Physical Universe."

The *Anunnaki* are described on the *Arcane Tablets* as "*primordial spirits*"—meaning that they already exist at the **inception** of the *ordered* Physical Universe. They choose to conquer the Physical Universe, *ordering* it to suit their own inhabitant survival after projecting their *Lifeline* of *Spirit* into physical forms. This is no small feat, but it is this very **premise** that originally defined "Divinity" or what we call "gods" in ancient times. We do not have a description of "why" *Alpha* beings operating from a Spiritual Universe would choose to infuse their *Lifeline* onto a *beta* physical existence in the Physical Universe—unless of course it is somehow evolutionary to the continued existence and survival of their *Alpha* state. We may conclude that the ultimate goal of survival as *Self* is spiritual immortality, which may in some unknown way be reflected in our ***beta existence*** and its ability to assist us in achieving our highest energetic state. As is stated in an esoteric "*Doctrine of Analogy*"—There is a **correspondence** between things *seen* and *unseen*; earth is the shadow of heaven and man is a reflection of divinity.*

> ***beta (existence)*** : "all manifestation in the 'Physical Universe' (**KI**); the 'Physical' state of existence consisting of **vibrations** of physical energy and physical matter moving through physical **space** and experienced as '**time**'; the *Awareness* of the *Alpha-spirit* (*Self*) as a physical **organic** *Lifeform* or *'genetic vehicle'* in which it experiences causality in the 'Physical Universe'."

* Quoting mystic philosopher, Eliphas Levi.

Even as a form of recreation, it would involve physical perception of motion for an otherwise spiritual or **static** existence—much like operating a remote "avatar" or a "virtual reality" experience from a stationary point. In fact, over the last several decades, as our understanding of these technologies has risen, we witness increased **consideration** of such paradigms, particularly in popular movies. The operator supplies the "***Will***" for causation—all of the **motor functions** and *beta* interactions are carried out and calculable within the parameters of physical experience.

It would seem that the *Anunnaki* had *quite a go of it* in the beginning, crashing about in the unfamiliar Physical Universe of physical solids and physical forces—enough **turbulence** to stir up a recourse action from the Law, when *Tiamat* dispenses the "*Tablets of Destiny*" with *Kingu*, the messenger action of the Law, across the Physical Universe. Therefore our first brush with the *Anunnaki* "gods" from the *Arcane Tablets* depicts them as spiritual *Lifeforms* **incarnate** in physical bodies engaged in an effort of dynamic conquest over the Physical Universe for their physical survival and existence. And what a picture that paints for us—for what loftier purpose for *Life* can we glean from this lore than that it *exists* and makes every effort to continue that *existence* to achieve the highest possible goal relative to all universes and possible existences, which is an increased *Awareness* that may earn a being ***Infinite Existence*** as a *Self-directed Spirit*. In that state, we are resuming **actualization** of our true **static** spiritual *Alpha* point of ***Self-Determinism***—and we may **enact** this *Awareness* upon our ***beta* existence** in the Physical Universe (**KI**).

Within the "Mardukite paradigm" shared among ancient Babylonian elite, Marduk had acquired the *True Knowingness* from the "*Tablets of Destiny*," which he then shared, demonstrating a map—a "spiritual pathway" through the turbulent Physical Universe—leading the way for *Lifeforms* occupying a physical existence on Earth to overcome disorienting distortions of a *beta* existence and everything that comes with it.

If we follow the *Pathway* appropriately to *Self-Honesty*, we ensure progress of our own existence by regaining the highest levels of our true "spiritual" ***Self*-actualized** *Awareness* while still operating in the Physical Universe. Such an accomplishment is our birthright—a true realization of ***God-hood*** in this *Lifetime* and proper ***Ascension*** of our *Spirit* thereafter, and its ability to rise up from the primal **dross** and walk among the *gods* in the *heavens* as one of them.

THE "BETA-AWARENESS TEST" ("BAT")

PURPOSE:

The "***Beta Awareness** Test*" ***(BAT)*** was developed for *Mardukite Systemology* to determine a "basic" or "average" state of personal *Awareness*—specifically: *Beta-Awareness* maintained by an individual *Alpha-Spirit* in its management of a *genetic-vehicle* to experience *beta-existence.*

A personal assessment of each "test" statement is rated and scored with an "**assessment scale**" based on the systematic relationship demonstrated by the *NexGen Systemology Standard Model*, first introduced in "*Tablets of Destiny*."

Additional ***psychometric evaluation*** of this assessment allows an individual to "chart" personal *Awareness **(ZU)*** according to "degrees" graphically demonstrated by the ***ZU-line*** (combined with the *Standard Model*) using the "average" ***BAT*** score.

INSTRUCTIONS:

Being as *honest* as you are able, complete each of the following statements using the *Assessment Scale* provided. With a pencil, write down the "number" (*numeric value*) from the *Assessment Scale next* to each statement. [Mark a "2" if you honestly "don't know" or are really uncertain.]

Don't be alarmed if you find many of the *assessment values* to be lower at first. The basic goal of ***NexGen Systemology*** is to increase certainty and ability for all of the qualities listed in the questionnaire.

You will assess the same "*Basic Awareness Test*" *(BAT)* several times while on the *Pathway to Self-Honesty* to chart your progress using *Mardukite Systemology Tech.* You may prefer to mark your answers directly onto the worksheet provided for evaluation.

Use a "*Self-Evaluation Test (SET) Worksheet*" the first time you read this far in the present book. Only include *numeric values* when testing to make certain you are not inadvertently performing "self-hypnosis" or ***autosuggestion**** using inadequate affirmations during *Self-Evaluation.*

---

* If an individual so desired, these statements *could be* reworked as positive affirmations, by inserting the most idealistic statement of "always" in each. However, such should not be performed as a substitution for true *Self-Evaluation.* Doing so could greatly hinder *actualized* progress on the *Pathway to Self-Honesty.*

THE NEXGEN SYSTEMOLOGY SELF-EVALUATION QUESTIONNAIRE

A-1 ___ = I am ___ successful at physical activities.

B-1 ___ = I ___ maintain control of my emotions.

C-1 ___ = I am ___ certain of what I know.

D-1 ___ = I am ___ in control of my reality.

E-1 ___ = I ___ make choices easily.

F-1 ___ = I am ___ understood by others.

G-1 ___ = I ___ find my life experience to be pleasurable.

H-1 ___ = I am ___ satisfied with my accomplishments.

I-1 ___ = I ___ solve my problems with goals and life successfully.

J-1 ___ = I ___ appreciate beauty in life, nature and the universe.

K-1 ___ = I ___ express myself warmly and cheerfully.

L-1 ___ = I ___ provide my highest quality of work.

M-1 ___ = I ___ take responsibility easily.

N-1 ___ = I am ___ respectful of traditions and opinions of others.

O-1 ___ = I am ___ sensitive to needs of others without succumbing to sympathetic emotion.

P-1 ___ = I am ___ cooperative and successful in a group.

ASSESSMENT SCALE
0 = Never
1 = Rarely
1.5 = Seldom
2 = Sometimes
2.5 = Usually
3 = Very Often
3.5 = Consistently
4 = Always

Q-1 ___ = I ___ know and trust myself, even in times of stress.

A-2 ___ = I ___ maintain my physical health and well-being.

B-2 ___ = I ___ maintain my composure when others are excited.

C-2 ___ = I ___ freely determine where to set my attentions and interests.

D-2 ___ = I am ___ the cause of my thoughts, ideas and emotions.

E-2 ___ = I ___ promptly make good decisions.

F-2 ___ = I ___ find it easy to communicate my thoughts and feelings to others.

G-2 ___ = I am ___ in control of my life.

H-2 ___ = I am ___ enthusiastic about my life and treat it as an adventure.

I-2 ___ = I ___ achieve my goals and objectives.

J-2 ___ = I ___ take quality time for myself, quietly, to think.

K-2 ___ = I ___ express my thoughts, feelings and abilities easily, openly and honestly.

L-2 ___ = I ___ consider effects of my decisions on others.

M-2 ___ = I ___ take responsibility for my emotional state.

N-2 ___ = I am ___ tolerant to beliefs of others.

O-2 ___ = I am ___ empathic to emotions of others without taking them on as my own.

P-2 ___ = I ___ set reasonable standards for myself and others.

Q-2 ___ = I ___ keep promises and repay debts.

A-3 ___ = I am ___ able to maintain good health, even when others in my environment are ill.

B-3 ___ = I ___ maintain my emotions and reactions under stress.

C-3 ___ = I can ___ change my mind, decisions or beliefs easily.

D-3 ___ = I am ___ able to manage my environment.

E-3 ___ = I ___ act to resolve a problem when I see it.

F-3 ___ = I ___ understand anything I decide to learn.

G-3 ___ = I am ___ in healthy and clean physical condition.

H-3 ___ = I am ___ content with my status and progress in life.

I-3 ___ = I ___ enjoy thinking about my future.

J-3 ___ = I am ___ able to enjoy my solitude.

K-3 ___ = I ___ exchange, express and receive ideas freely, openly and easily.

ASSESSMENT SCALE

0	= Never
1	= Rarely
1.5	= Seldom
2	= Sometimes
2.5	= Usually
3	= Very Often
3.5	= Consistently
4	= Always

L-3 ___ = I ___ gain trust and support from others with my enthusiasm.

M-3 ___ = I ___ take responsibility for my thoughts and actions.

N-3 ___ = I ___ conduct myself without resentment.

O-3 ___ = I am ___ able to assist someone in need without becoming emotional.

P-3 ___ = I ___ consider what happens to others.

Q-3 ___ = I ___ meet my obligations and fulfill promises.

A-4 ___ = I ___ keep my possessions neat and orderly

B-4 ___ = I ___ avoid feeling gloomy and depressed.

C-4 ___ = I ___ think clearly in intense, emotional or stressful situations.

D-4 ___ = I ___ affect those in my environment with my thoughts and emotions.

E-4 ___ = I ___ act to resolve needless suffering when I see it.

F-4 ___ = I ___ know when to speak—and when to remain silent

G-4 ___ = I ___ calculate risks effectively before I act.

H-4 ___ = I am ___ able to adapt to any situation.

I-4 ___ = I ___ set future goals and achieve them.

J-4 ___ = I am ___ able to clearly *imagine* images/sounds/smells/any sensation that I have *not* experienced.

K-4 ___ = I am ___ able to express my affections.

L-4 ___ = I ___ can find something to be enthusiastic about.

M-4 ___ = I ___ maintain control of my time management.

N-4 ___ = I am ___ patient in my interactions with others.

O-4 ___ = I ___ can sense when others silently react or (mis)understand my communications.

P-4 ___ = I am ___ sought by others for advice and counsel.

Q-4 ___ = I ___ determine the truth of matters I am interested in.

A-5 ___ = I ___ appreciate and take care of my property.

B-5 ___ = I ___ put emotional memories aside when solving present problems or working toward future goals.

C-5 ___ = I ___ can recall past events clearly and vividly.

D-5 ___ = I ___ make every effort to fully utilize and advance my knowledge and ability.

E-5 ___ = I ___ continue a task to completion, even if I make mistakes.

F-5 ___ = I ___ find out the information when I do not fully understand something.

G-5 ___ = I am ___ able to clearly *recall* images/sounds/smells/any sensation that I *have* experienced in the past.

H-5 ___ = I ___ can fully focus my concentration on the present task at hand.

I-5 ___ = I am ___ courageous, upfront and forthcoming in my behavior.

J-5 ___ = I ___ occupy my time and efforts creating, building or designing something.

K-5 ___ = I ___ share my thoughts and ideas with others.

ASSESSMENT SCALE
0 = Never
1 = Rarely
1.5 = Seldom
2 = Sometimes
2.5 = Usually
3 = Very Often
3.5 = Consistently
4 = Always

L-5 ___ = I am ___ considered a cheerful person by others.

M-5 ___ = I ___ can cause change in my environment at will.

N-5 ___ = I ___ can receive criticism from others without exhibiting an emotional reaction.

O-5 ___ = I ___ assist others to understand when my communication is misunderstood.

P-5 ___ = I am ___ considered dependable by others.

Q-5 ___ = I am ___ truthful and honest to myself and others.

A-6 ___ = I ___ take care of, maintain and treat my physical environment well.

B-6 ___ = I ___ *sense* an emotional state before I *feel* it.

C-6 ___ = I ___ think positive thoughts about myself and others.

D-6 ___ = I ___ think and act systematically.

E-6 ___ = I ___ have close friends I can confide in.

F-6 ___ = I ___ seek to improve an ability or increase a skill.

G-6 ___ = I am ___ able to discard old memorabilia freely.

H-6 ___ = I ___ avoid borrowing money or using credit cards.

I-6 ___ = I ___ act to protect and maintain our planet and ecosystem on earth.

J-6 ___ = I am ___ able to create new things and develop new ideas.

K-6 ___ = I ___ can motivate others to action.

L-6 ___ = I am ___ considered charismatic by others.

M-6 ___ = I ___ control the urge for excess or to overindulge.

N-6 ___ = I ___ restrain my display of anger toward others.

O-6 ___ = I am ___ welcoming to the company of children and animals.

P-6 ___ = I ___ keep my office/study neat and organized.

Q-6 ___ = I am ___ considered trustworthy by others.

SELF-ANALYSIS

This "*Beta-Awareness Test*" *(BAT)* may be scored and evaluated—or *analyzed*—in several ways.

The most basic method of evaluation also carries the most advanced requirement—an experienced *NexGen Systemologist* with sufficient knowledge of the subject and *Awareness Chart* to plot a score for themselves using just a few key **assessments** that are known with certainty.

The standard method requires you to write down a *numeric assessment value* for each statement directly onto a "*Self-Evaluation Test (SET) Worksheet*"—as provided. There is a space on the worksheet for all key pieces of information: each *individual answer*; the totals and averages for answered *rows* (such as "A"); and the total and average of a *completed* worksheet.

> STEP #1: Begin with the value for "A-1" and proceed to the space below it for "B-1" and so on. At the end of the questionnaire, you will have completed—and assigned values to—approximately 100 statements. Once these values are all marked on the worksheet, certain observations or **patterns** may already become **apparent**—but we make further calculations anyway.

For example: it may become obvious when any particular value—such as "2.0" or "2.5"—appears more frequently than any other, thus somewhat accurately representing the total average itself; or it may be noticed that all values contained within certain rows are significantly higher or lower than those found in other rows—thus somewhat accurately representing particular areas of ability and deficiency reflected in a ***Seeker's*** current or present state of *Awareness*.

> STEP #2: We effectively seek (and accurately use) "averages" for evaluation because specific "qualities" addressed in the questionnaire—as systematized in

> each *row*—each have a strong tendency to "rise and fall" together. Likewise, the "total average" for a completed worksheet may be used to plot a *Seeker's* base "level" on the *Awareness Chart*, because all of these "qualities" are also systematically interconnected—thus quite accurately representing an overall demonstration of the *Seeker's* personal management of *Reality Experience* in *Self-Honesty*.

TOTALS for a *row* (A-1 + A-2 + A-3...) may be marked on the worksheet at the end of the row. There is also a space for the option of calculating the row AVERAGE. If you have difficulty calculating the AVERAGE for rows, don't worry. Simply add up the TOTAL of each row to write in the "TOTAL" column for that row and skip to *Step #3*. The TOTAL of each row is more important for overall completed test accuracy than an individual row AVERAGE, which you may estimate as needed.

It is true that the *exact* AVERAGE for a row is equal to the TOTAL of its six values *divided* by six—but this is *not* necessary. If all of the values in a row are the same, than the AVERAGE will be the same—or, if a certain value appears most often, you can simply use that value as an AVERAGE estimation for the row.

> STEP #3: A *completed test* is quite simple to score and evaluate. Write the TOTAL for the "*SET Worksheet*" by adding up the *column* of values for each individual row TOTAL. In most cases, this provides a three-digit or three-figure value, meaning in the hundreds. Because we have approximately 100 questions or values, the completed test AVERAGE is easily calculated by moving two "decimal places" of the TOTAL. For example: a completed *test total of 220* (*220.*) would be scored as an *average of 2.2* (*2.20*) on the *Awareness Chart*. Or—a completed *test total of 318* would equal an *average of 3.18* on the *Chart*, or *3.2* if we want to "round" for convenience.

Self-Evalutation Test (SET) Worksheet

(Use a pencil to reuse this worksheet.)

	1	2	3	4	5	6	TOTAL 1-6	AVG.
A								
B								
C								
D								
E								
F								
G								
H								
I								
J								
K								
L								
M								
N								
O								
P								
Q								
							TOT ____	AVG ____

After average scores are determined, a closer examination of the "*Beta Awareness Test*" *(BAT)* and completed "*Self-Evaluation Test Worksheet*" *(SET)* reveals additional data for *advanced* Self-Analysis.

It will be noticed that questionnaire statements demonstrate a pattern. There are many reasons *why* our questionnaire is arranged as it is—however, it is much more important for the *Seeker* to understand *how* it is arranged—*after* it is completed the first time.

Letters "A" through "Q" are assigned to statements on the *BAT* questionnaire. There are *six* cycles of these, composing a complete *row* on the *SET* worksheet. Each *row* represents a particular *category*. Each of these categories reflects traits indicative of a specific "**personality** *quality*" or "*aspect of Self* in *beta experience*" that may be evaluated independently —and in systematic relation to the others—with *advanced Self-analysis*.

These categories are distinguished by the following aspects:

SELF-EVALUATION TEST ASPECTS

A = Managing Physical Conditions
B = Managing Emotional Energy
C = Managing Thought Activity
D = Managing External Reality Environment
E = Managing Choice & Decision
F = Managing Communication & Understanding
G = Managing the Past
H = Managing the Present
I = Managing the Future
J = Managing Imagination & Creation
K = Managing Personal Expression (To Others)
L = Managing Personal Magnetism
M = Managing Responsibility & Self-Control
N = Managing Personal Tolerance (To Others)
O = Managing Assistance & Sympathy (To Others)
P = Managing Interpersonal Organization
Q = Managing Self-Honesty

The first questionnaire statement for each category (A-1, B-1, *&tc.*) is a personal assessment of an upper-most expression, consequence or "the *effect*" regarding that aspect. A perfectly executed honest test—in theory—would result in an *average value* for the *row* being equivalent to this answer alone. However, we are aware of many shortcomings inherent in any method of subjective analysis, especially when it comes to ourselves. Therefore, it is critical—for a systematic approach—that we balance or *average* out any *mathematical* evaluation with "*reason*" if we are to effectively plot it on an "**objective" gradient**—such as the *Awareness Scale*.

"Blanket statements" are sometimes challenging for an individual to determine for themselves. As a result, we provide the *Seeker* some leeway here by offering five additional ***causative*** *statements* to average out a complete assessment. Each subsequent statement within a category, after the first, assesses personal "*cause*"—the degree of ***Self-determination*** yielding the results or *effects* for that aspect as *beta experience*.

For example: in the first "A-statement" we assess very simply a generalization of how successful we are in physical activities. Each subsequent "A-statement" refers to *Self-directed reasons* why we may be at *that* level of "success" in physical activities—mainly how we treat our body, our physical possessions and manage our immediate physical environment. We should expect *values* to be the same or similar, but since tests and experiments are not written or conducted under absolute (or perfect) **conditions**, we calculate averages for our purposes—and the results seem to be consistent.

While developing this test, we discovered that category types evaluated here all share a very interesting attribute in common. They are all the *subject* and *basis* of nearly every *applied* form of "spirituality," "mysticism," or "religious prayer"—essentially any "magical" property or aspect we might wish to *attract* greater "certainty" and "**control**" of in our ***beta existence***. Yet, we soon discover that *all* of these "domains" are inherently *our* "domains" to be **responsible** for. The actualization of *Self-Honesty* toward directing and "managing" *beta existence* is conditional on—and **proportional** to—the personal responsibility for *acquiring* "right education" and *applying* "right effort" in each of these categories.

It is important that a *Seeker* is able to clearly evaluate the data from a completed "*SET*" worksheet. Each time a "*SET*" worksheet is completed, a *Seeker* can mark *averages* for each *row*/category on the following worksheet addendum titled: "*Self-Evaluation Test (SET) Analysis Summary.*" This data can be easily plotted on a graph (provided). There is also space allotted next to each "category description" for additional notes.

Self-Evaluation Test (SET) Analysis Summary

(Use a pencil to reuse this worksheet.)

	AVERAGE	CATEGORY
A		Physical Condition
B		Emotional Energy
C		Thought Activity
D		External Reality Environment
E		Choice & Decision Making
F		Communication & Understanding
G		Managing the Past
H		Managing the Present
I		Managing the Future
J		Imagination & Creation
K		Personal Expression to Others
L		Personal Magnetism
M		Responsibility & Self-Control
N		Personal Tolerance to Others
O		Assistance & Sympathy to Others
P		Interpersonal Organization
Q		Managing Self-Honesty
‡		BETA AWARENESS TEST SCORE

Self-Evaluation Test (SET) Analysis Graph

(Use different colors to graph changes on this addendum.)

‡	A	B	C	D	E	F	G	H	I	J	K	L	M	N	O	P	Q	%
4																		100
3.5																		85
3																		70
2.5																		55
2																		40
1.5																		25
1																		10
0.5																		5
0.1																		1
‡	A	B	C	D	E	F	G	H	I	J	K	L	M	N	O	P	Q	%

THE "STANDARD MODEL" OF SYSTEMOLOGY

Intensive analysis of ancient "*cuneiform tablets*" from **Mesopotamia** led to our development of the "Standard Model of Systemology"—accounted for in the volume, Tablets of Destiny, also referred to in Mardukite Systemology as "*Liber-One.*" Early research and experimentation using Systemology: The Original Thesis also led to a discovery and understanding of "**ZU**"—or more specifically, the "***ZU-line***"—and its significance for developing *NexGen Systemology* into an "*applied spiritual philosophy*" that is now communicable and effective.

Our *Pathway to Self-Honesty* in *Mardukite Systemology* is demonstrated with the "Standard Model." The **gradient** scale by which we chart anything on this *model*—in relation to *Self-Awareness*—is defined as the "ZU-line"—which is a graphic representation of the spiritual energy frequency that we call *Awareness* (or ***consciousness***) imbuing all *Life*. This "ZU" energy originates in the "Spiritual Universe" ("**AN**") as the "I" or "*Self*." It extends from this *Alpha* state as "spirit" to the "Physical Universe" ("**KI**") where it maintains a *beta* state by controlling an "**organic**/genetic body."

> It is the range of ***beta existence***—and our interaction with the Physical Universe (**KI**) as *Actualized Awareness*—that we are most concerned with at this level of (*Grade-III Systemology*) work with the *Standard Model*.

We effectively chart all *degrees* of ZU *fragmentation* pertaining to the range of concentrated THOUGHT energy frequencies between (2.0) and (4.0) on the *Standard Model*.

—AND—

These may be even more deeply cemented as our Reality—by a combination of efforts and forces—as *encoded* ***imprints*** in the energy range of EMOTION between (0.0) and (2.0).

The "*Awareness Scale*"—or more accurately, the "***Beta Awareness*** *Scale*"—emphasizes specifically the *beta* range of the *Standard Model*, the degrees between (0.0) and (4.0); as does our simplified version of it, called the "*Emotimeter.*"

The *(Beta) Awareness Scale* demonstrates all degrees of personal **ZU** that fall between two states: a fully expressed total "***Self-Actualized***" *beta-Awareness* at (4.0); and organic death of the physical body at (0.0). It as at (4.0) that we refer to a *Seeker* as having reached a ***defragmented*** state equivalent to the most basic level of personal *Actualization* in *Self-Honesty*, which is "*beta.*" This is actually what we are "testing" with a *BAT*—and evaluating with *SET* worksheets.

The easiest way to understand this approach—and integrate an understanding of the *Awareness Scale* as applied knowledge—is by introducing the subject of the "*Emotimeter.*" What we are calling the "*Emotimeter*" is essentially a simplified version of our complete (*Beta) Awareness Scale*. Both the *Emotimeter* and *(Beta) Awareness Scale* may be applied to existing **knowledge** of the "*Standard Model of Systemology*" and the "***ZU-line***" relayed in <u>Tablets of Destiny</u>.

NEXGEN SYSTEMOLOGY "EMOTIMETER"

<u>4</u> = Full Awareness Expressed ("Vibrant")
<u>3.5</u> = Outgoing/Pointed ("Positive")
<u>3</u> = Content/Friendly ("Casual")
<u>2.5</u> = Tolerant ("Dismissive")
<u>2</u> = Suspicious ("Pessimistic")
<u>1.5</u> = Violent/Spiteful ("Negative")
<u>1</u> = Evasive ("Afraid")
<u>0.5</u> = Grieving ("Sad")
<u>0.1</u> = Apathetic ("Unconscious")
<u>0</u> = Organic Death/Physical Universe (KI)

The *Emotimeter* can be used to evaluate a considerable wealth of information even without incorporating further divisions and descriptions charted by the full *Awareness Scale*. The previous *Assessment Scale* given to evaluate *BAT* questionnaire statements is directly based on the *Emotimeter*. Therefore, a *Seeker* may use this to analyze basic data provided on a completed *SET* worksheet and addenda.

Some particular details became clear to us with our new understanding of *beta-Awareness*. For one: it became evident that the basic states described by the *Emotimeter* mirrored **conditions** of "*havingness*" and attainment of "*knowingness*" reflected in traditional approaches to "*Self-Actualization*" maintained by a few **humanist**-motivational schools of contemporary psychology. It will also be recognized, by anyone with previous familiarity on such topics, that *NexGen Systemology* is advancing an understanding beyond what has already been laid out—with an "application" of knowledge into a more workable methodology carrying effective idealistic goals for the "common man."

At the frequency degree of "personal fear" (1.0), an individual is only seeking information, or data from their environment, in order to simply *cope* with Reality in a primitive sense. At this level of *Awareness*, the motivation to "exist" is driven by resolving the most basic survival needs only. Of course, at this level of *Awareness* an individual is less likely to actually be successful in having these needs met by their own efforts and actions. In fact, this **condition** can be extended all the way up to (2.0). This is because the ability to *be, know* and *act* as *Self-directed* from the "I" as the *Alpha* "*Self*" significantly diminishes the "further down" in degree we are on any *Scale* based on the *Standard Model*.

Assuming basic needs are met, a person at (2.0) is no longer maintaining an active state of fear or anger toward their environment. They may therefore look to fulfill the next level of basic need: *security*. In essence, once an individual figures out how to establish its basic needs, the next logical effort is to maintain them—and so they seek the information and resources from their environment that will *assist* them in achieving a foundation of stability. Such stability promotes further expansion and longevity of personal existence. At its most fundamental and biological core, this would include specifically *family* and our closest ties to other *Lifeforms* that *assist* us in our continued existence.

A society between (2.0) and (2.5) is only interested in promoting and maintaining the most basic needs of an individual—which keeps the average population in a state somewhere between "pessimistic suspicion" and "dismissive tolerance" at best. Not very *enlightening*. The theme of society is: As long as people are not simply running amok, everything's fine.

We therefore do not see a drive toward any greater *enlightenment* or any larger effective group dynamic taking place until we reach approximately (3.0). It is at (3.0) that we begin to see signs of a healthy interest in *Life* and general existence. After physical conditions are **relatively** stable and there is a firm foundation for expansion, an individual's *beta-Awareness* is usually free and unwound enough from past and present concerns to pursue higher interests. This does not mean they will automatically **discern** only correct knowledge, or that they will be successful in all their endeavors, but the *interest* is there at a level we would consider at least somewhat *above* normal average.

An individual coming up to (3.0) for the first time is just beginning to truly *reason* for themselves. This individual could be book-smart, but they might also be overly cautious or conservative in accepting *any* information as facts. They might find many things interesting, but may still treat all data equally and casually. At the very least, a person at (3.0) is simply in the *know* that there is *something* "true" to *know*. They are becoming *Aware* that they are *Aware* and that there are things to be *Aware* of *Self-Honestly*. This seems trite—and yet it is considered above average to current societal norms.

If a *Seeker* is first discovering the *Mardukite* work, *Systemology* and the *Pathway to Self-Honesty* from subjectively lower points on the *Emotimeter*, it is when they elevate to (3.0) that they usually begin to notice the greatest *shift* between a point they were coming from and where they are headed. This state is sometimes achieved relatively quickly after applying basics of *Systemology* ***Processing*** and education for even a short time. The gradient "slope" between (3.0) and (4.0) is generally determined by the individual, their application of the principles and the amount of personal *fragmentation* remaining to be resolved in the form of **erroneous** "*emotional* ***imprints***" and "***thought-formed*** *beliefs*."

At higher levels of *beta-Awareness*—such as from (3.5) to (4.0)—an individual has already managed their past *imprints* and is managing present issues quite well. There have been many successful individuals and personalities in history that appear to regularly maintain these levels innately. This is what allows true *visionaries* and *leaders* to set their **attentions** and *Awareness* on the *future*, rather than being fixed to past or present problems. As such, we tend to find a motivation for *empowerment* occurring at this level—whether or not it is supplemented by *Self-Honesty*.

Systemology education and higher-level ***processing*** techniques become increasingly critical for development when a *Seeker* experiences higher rates of personal **vibration** or ***ZU**-frequency*. Once a *Seeker* has rehabilitated their identification (*realization*) of the *Alpha Spirit* or *Self*, the goal is quite simply to make the able *more able*. Up to this point in the program—as demonstrated within the present volume—the method is simply for a *Seeker* to work a little further and a little further to essentially achieve this baseline *Awareness* where "the real work"—the actualized *Alpha* work—can begin. It is at a point of "free expression" that we can focus on *what* exactly we are expressing. Because this is important—hence: education.

A person could be elevated to a point of sheer outward vibrancy and charisma *without* actually achieving a true *beta*-state of *Self-Honesty*.* The two states are clearly not the same; they simply resonate similarly by external observation. If we consider "basic needs" data from Abraham Mas-

---

* In *Systemology*, this is called "Grandeur" or the "*false Four*."

low's "*Pyramid of Self-Actualization*" in relation to (1.0) to (4.0) on the *Standard Model*:

DYNAMICS OF BASIC NEEDS & BETA SURVIVAL

4 = Humanity; success; personal esteem.
3 = Group interaction; purpose.
2 = Family unit; domestic security.
1 = Self; **physiology**; primitive survival.

—we can arrive at many effective parallels between. An individual generally occupies a *level* of *beta-Awareness* consistent with a level of the Physical Universe **(KI)** they have achieved personal *mastery* of. By this "*mastery*" we *do not* mean some exercise of blatant (and ignorant) totalitarian control. We mean a level of "*mastery*" in the same fashion that an artist *masters* their craft. And we can be certain that the "crafting of universes" *is* an art-form (as much as it is cold science and logic) of which we are **participating** in by our *agreements* of Reality at every moment. This is the knowledge that constitutes our *Standard Model*—deciphered from secrets kept in the oldest libraries of Mesopotamia, forged at the **inception** of modern civilization and the original systematization of the modern *Human Condition*.

In fact the *Standard Model* and our "quantification" (or *numeric values*) of the ***ZU-line*** would not be nearly as useful to us if it could not be directly related to other current valid data somewhere within its range to "know" things. This is because our *Standard Model* is a "*continuity model*," which has been demonstrated in Tablets of Destiny to include *Everything* and *Nothing* from *Infinity-to-Infinity*. It is evident by our application of the *Emotimeter* to states of the Human Condition, that this model is applicable in demonstrating both the *subjective* and ***objective*** Universe—especially as we experience it in *beta existence*—and that it reflects a perfected map by which a person might navigate the ***Game*** of this Physical Universe and reach the *Pathway of Self-Honesty*.

The *Emotimeter* simplifies the more complete *(Beta) Awareness Scale*, developed from an intensive understanding of the *ZU-line*—when metered or gauged alongside the *Standard Model*. Our efforts did not result from *complicating* knowledge into a larger more complete scale; we developed the deepest understanding possible and then reduced it to a simplification. Our "true understanding" as "true knowledge" should always be in the direction of reduction: a wide range of valid data brought to a point or spark of *true knowing*. There is no reason to over-complicate a system unless its designers are set out for ***authoritarian*** *control*—in which the artificial convolution is allegedly only understood by a select few "*authorities*."

Our own intentions within *Mardukite Systemology* are only to distribute a complete **holistic** understanding as it has been, and continues to be, discovered; *Graded* or ***tiered*** by educational levels only so it may be realized into "true knowledge" with the greatest certainty, and not simply in some **esoteric** attempts at cryptic delivery.

The "*Ancient Mystery School*"—from which our founding data is drawn—also conducted itself in a cumulative manner, carrying *Seekers* through initiatory degrees. In essence, the best route to learning is often conducted in this way—so long as the material is applicably *graded* specific to the individual. This is not always easy to arrange as a "static book." Grade-I and Grade-II apprenticeship programs (under an authorized *Mardukite Master*) are also currently in development—in addition to a ***Piloting*** *Program* aimed at preparing professionals to deliver "Grade III" (and above) *NexGen Systemology* ***Processing***. All of this is aimed toward greater quality assistance to *the individual* as this movement and organization progresses into the future with its goals of global *spiritual transhumanism* ("spiritual metahumanism") leading toward a new Human evolution: the state of ***Homo Novus***.

For those *Seekers* continuing on to this material from *Liber-One (Tablets of Destiny)*, it will be noted that "***Processing***" in this book is primarily concerned with actualizing the portion of the *ZU-line* (and *Standard Model*) that directly relates to *beta-existence* in the Physical Universe—sometimes referred to as "**KI**" in ***Mardukite Zuism***, as derived from a **Sumerian *cuneiform sign*** for the "material world" and planet Earth. This *beta* range of personal ***ZU-frequency*** **vibration** interacting with the Physical Universe (**KI**) as *Life in Awareness (**ZU**)*, is plotted between two points:

a.) the point of densest most inert physical matter at (0.0) or *KI*; and

b.) the point at which the *Alpha Spirit* of the "*I*" of-and-as "*Self*" contacts systems of the *genetic vehicle* that it controls, or is **anchored** to, at (4.0).

Between (0.0) and (4.0) are various *beta states* of *fragmentation* inherent in a *Seeker's* **participation** in *beta-existence* as the Human Condition. These *genetic vehicles* are actually quite amazing bodies to have use of while interacting with the Physical Universe (KI). They may not be necessary, but they are convenient to have use of while we work up to the research and actualized states that will allow us to move between them *at will*. Unfortunately, without this knowledge, as an individual becomes more and more the *effect* of this Physical Universe—and thereby less of a *Self-Honest Cause* to Reality—all *fragmentation* thickens, erroneous ***Imprints*** become deeper, more numerous, and ***thought-forms*** become more solid.

This phenomenon tends to happen with "age"—as an individual agreeing to the Human Condition accumulates more and more of this *reactive programming*. This can also happen throughout the course of a lifetime with the accumulation of painful experiences—and potentially even carried through many lifetimes. As a result, *Awareness* moves down the *Emotimeter* or *Scale*—primitive "reactive behavior" concerning basic needs and securities of preserving physical existence begin to take over and **displace** *Alpha Awareness*. An individual first begins to *react* "as a wild, sick or injured animal"—and then at even lower levels of *Awareness*, falls into an apathetic "near death" state of hopelessness.

Personal states described on the *Emotimeter, (Beta) Awareness Scale*—or directly on the *ZU-line*—concern ***objective*** frequencies and **vibrations** that are experienced *subjectively.* They are derived from basic logic and observed universal mathematics. This means that the highest **band** of *beta-Awareness* between (3.8) and (4.0) could include any states reached as personal "peak experiences" of a *Seeker's* lifetime —points of greatest achievement and milestones of utmost success that are the apex of human experience and "ecstasy" when we are "walking on air" seemingly "outside of ourselves" (*ex-stasis*) *&tc.*

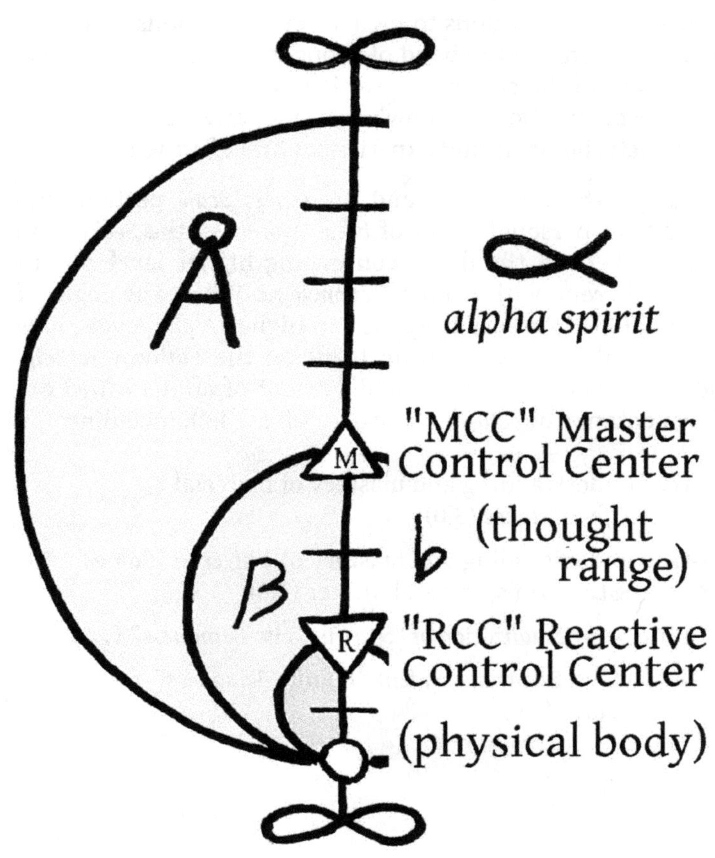

We say that our quantitative (*numeric approach*) to *beta-Awareness* does not concern "*existentials*" because it says nothing directly of whether or not *Self-Honesty* is *actually* maintained at these peak points—or of an individual's ability to maintain this "peak elation" as *fully Actualized beta-Awareness* thereafter. Of course we are not seeking some "external event" to spark a change in us—but the "peak experience" similarity is the best relative equation we may provide to a *Seeker* at this time. In essence, a *Seeker* that is elevated to higher levels of *beta-Awareness* would have resolved their personal management of the basic securities related to material "*Havingness*" and would therefore be moving their attentions to higher demonstrations of Reality activity *realized* in the band of thought vibration as *Knowing* or a state of "*Knowingness*"—which is not the same as the sheer accumulation of knowledge, but rather a *reduction* of data, facts, imprints and experiences into *effective truth*.

Although the *Emotimeter* and *Awareness Scale* pertain specifically to personal states of *beta-Awareness*, the *Seeker* will not be "kept in the dark" concerning higher level **potentials** inherent within our *Systemology*. When the logic of personal ***ZU-frequency*** is applied to higher *Alpha* levels, new theoretical avenues open up to us on the *Pathway to Self-Honesty*—even beyond the achievement of an *Actualized* **defragmentation** of *beta-Awareness* as *Self* at (4.0), including:

—true understanding and mastery of material *Life-Existence* (5.0);

—true understanding and mastery of *Universes, **Games** & Logics* of spirit and matter (6.0);

—total *Self-Actualization of "Spiritual Life-Beingness"* (7.0);

—actualized *Self-transcendent "Infinite Beingness" at Source* (8.0).

UNDERSTANDING SCALES AND DEGREES ON A CONTINUITY MODEL

An individual's *Lifeforce (or ZU)*, experienced as *Spiritual Awareness* of *Self*, is a constant force of ***Will*** set in action from a Source in Infinity. A lessening of total *Awareness*—and equally the actualization of *Self-Honesty*—in the experience of this *Lifetime*, is only a result of two things:

a.) turbulent emotional energy wound up in *encoded imprints*; and

b.) creative mental energy cemented in ***thought-formed*** *beliefs.*

The first (a) is primarily resolved with intensive *Systemology* ***Processing*** combined with *Self-Evaluation*; the second (b) is handled the same, combined with extensive *Systemology Education*, so that the reality of *thought-formed beliefs* and *encoded imprints* is better understood and managed in the future. The end goal of *Mardukite Systemology* is always in the direction of "*Self-reliance*" and not to promote some misguided emotional dependency on any religious organization or spiritual institution. Such methods were once tried by all carriers of some truth in the past; and as a result, all failed to deliver what they promised their *Seekers*.

One of the primary axioms of *NexGen Systemology* and ***Mardukite Zuism*** is that:

"The *Self* occupying the *genetic vehicle* is a 'spiritual universe cause' of 'physical universe effects' engaging a ***Self-determined*** Alpha-Spirit '**Will**' as *Actualized Awareness* in *beta existence.*"*

Consequently we can rate or quantify the *degree* or *level* of personal actualization chronically expressed in *beta-exist-*

---

* Excerpting fundamentals from "*Mardukite Zuism: A Brief Introduction*" and "*Tablets of Destiny*" by Joshua Free.

ence—on the *(Beta) Awareness Scale*—if we apply "percentage values" from the *(Set) Analysis Graph.*[‡]

Awareness is the best word we can used to apply to *ZU*. It is the definitive *Self* that is "conscious" as "I" when **controlling** a physical body; the *Self* that is ***Willing*** all sense of *doing, having, knowing* and *being*; and ultimately the *Alpha-Spiritual Self* that remains "I" even after a genetic death of the physical body it maintains control **anchors** with. *Awareness* is then more closely tied to our concept of personal *existence* than any other available. Hence the exhaustion of the use of the term throughout this book—and also *Self-Honesty*, which is the actualization of that *Awareness* free from **inhibitory** and reactive programming that **displaces** *Self* in managing interpretations and agreements of Reality.

The important thing to keep in mind whenever examining *degrees* and the *levels* of *Awareness* described within specific *parameters*, is that these are *scales* within said *parameters* and not systems being treated in isolation or exclusion to all other *macro-systems* and *micro-systems* active "above" and "below" wherever we are examining on the *ZU-continuum*. For our current purposes, we have chosen to focus our attentions specifically on factors directly related to *beta-Awareness* and our basic management of *Beta Existence*—the

---

‡ This is estimated with mathematical logic within the *Beta* range from the *Standard Model*. The full continuum for "*Infinity-to-Infinity*"—which must include everything *exterior* to *beta existence*—would extend not only from (8.0) to (0.0), but then also down to (–8.0). Personal experience of the "Physical Universe" only manifests within vibrations of the levels between (0.0) and (4.0), but this does not even exclude the possibility of other "Physical Universes" also existing at that frequency, which are spatially separated. The *Standard Model* does not actually prove this, since it is established from the perspective of "Self" in *this* "Physical Universe"—but it does not exclude the possibility. More of these considerations, which at this time may seem distracting, will be reserved for higher *Grades* of material.

"Reality" of the Physical Universe (**KI**).

Another important feature of the *Awareness Scale* is that it is a *subjective* representation of *objective* energy vibrations. It relates very precisely to general interactions between frequencies, but not the actual content communicated or complete validity of data **transmitted.** Yet we can be certain, for example, in the instance of an *Alpha-Spirit's* ability to form *imprints* that:

a.) lower levels relate to states of emotional turbulence and ***emotional encoding*** that generate those states of a destructive nature, contributing to a rejection of the Physical Universe; and

b.) higher (*beta*) states promote a personal motivation toward material success and achievement accomplished through effectively maintaining and transforming the Physical Universe with *thought-forms.*

We can apply many such "**dichotomies**" to the range of any scale we choose to apply to our *Standard Model*, so long as we understand that it is not a *finite dualistic* model, and that it actually extends in *degree* toward *Infinity* in directions or levels both "above" and "below" wherever we fix the parameters of a scale. For example, if we were to theoretically scale *Self-Determinism* of an *Alpha Spirit* on the *Standard Model*, it would run from 100% Infinite Cause (8.0) down to 100% Physical Effect (0.0). Of course, we only experience a portion of this **spectrum** within the *beta* range as *Awareness* using existing faculties of the Human Condition. Therefore, midway between we find the interaction between the *Alpha* and *beta* at (4.0), which is the key point of *Self-Honest* transmission between the *Alpha Spirit* and the Mind-Systems interacting with a *genetic body.*[∞] We could apply similar scales of "Right and Wrong" and "Always and Never"—or of any *positive* condition (its state of "*beingness*") or creation and at the other end, its state of *not-being.* This becomes in-

∞ This point at (4.0) is quite properly referred to as the *Master Control Center* or *MCC* in "*Tablets of Destiny.*"

creasingly evident with examination and study of the *Awareness Scale*.

As a *Seeker* increases their familiarity with various fundamentals of the Human Condition, they discover more about themselves and others—but as a variety of knowledge that leads to "*true understanding*," which must (by definition) also lend itself toward a mostly valid prediction of future results based on existing evaluations. Without such consistency, all we are left with is a vague idea—nothing of substance to base our *model* upon. Fortunately we have developed a strong *model* for our purposes, drawn out from thousands of years of humanity's research concerning *beta-experience* in addition to our own applications and experimental pursuits of *NexGen Systemology*.

Understanding and applying the *(Beta) Awareness Scale** allows an individual the best chance of understanding themselves and individuals around them. In addition we earn a greater understanding concerning our environment and our ability to manage it successfully. Some of these details become clearer—or with greater "reality"—during personal ***processing***.

The fundamental ***spectrum*** reflected in the *Emotimeter* and *Awareness Scale* is a description of the most basic *levels* of *beta-existence*—and personal *Awareness* of the same. The ideal basic state of the Human Condition operating from the *Alpha-Spirit* is marked at (4.0) on these charts. This is the point on the *Standard Model* that **differentiates** a frequency **threshold** between two distinct states:

a.) energy and matter of a "*Beta*" Physical Universe (**KI**); and

b.) energy and matter of an "*Alpha*" Spiritual Universe (**AN**).

On a personal level of existence, when we are dealing with degrees in the range of *beta*, we are referring not so much to

* Hereafter referred to simply as the "*Awareness Scale.*"

BETA-AWARENESS SCALE CHART

"4.0"	SELF-HONESTY (BASIC STATE)	(4.0) Charismatic
"3.9"	SUCCESS/ACHIEVEMENT	<
"3.8"	Elated/"In Love"	(3.8) Enthusiastic
		(3.6) Cheerful/Energetic
"3.5"	CONFIDENT	<
		(3.4) Determined/Eager
"3.2"	Strong Interest	(3.2) Vigorous/Alert
"3.0"	INTERESTED	<
"2.8"	Mild Interest	(2.8) Encouraged
		(2.6) Doubtful/Disinterest
"2.5"	INDIFFERENT	<
		(2.4) Bored/Tired
"2.1"	Monotony	(2.2) Neglect/Dislike
"2.0"	INVALIDATING	<
"1.8"	Pain Sensation	(1.8) Antagonism
		(1.6) Confrontation/Violence
"1.5"	ANGER	<
		(1.4) Hateful
"1.2"	Resentment	(1.2) Anxiety
"1.0"	FEAR	<
"0.8"	Numb	(0.8) Terror
		(0.6) Grief/Loss
"0.5"	SUFFERING	<
		(0.4) Depression
"0.2"	Victimization	(0.2) Hopelessness
"0.1"	APATHY	<
	Pretend Death	(0.05) Uselessness
"0.0"	INERT PHYSICAL UNIVERSE	(0.0) Organic Death

the frequencies of our environment, but those that relate specifically to our own expression and interaction (of ZU) with environmental energy. Thus we can better understand, for example, an individual communicating from any particular level of vibration that can produce effects in the environment and on others in that environment.

We see a range of physical interaction between (0.0) and (1.0) that is reduced to the most dense inert low energy physical matter. We can chart other emotional interactions between (1.0) and (2.0) that remain below the level of thought and reason and are primarily reactive-response mechanisms developed from *emotionally encoded imprints* of experience. Between (2.0) and (4.0) we plot all degrees of "*Thought*" activity and the expression of *Self* in the Physical Universe (**KI**). It is within *this* range of "Mind-Systems" that most *Processing* within this present volume is targeting.

This point of *Self-Honesty* we are *Seeking* in our work is not some newly concocted state that we have decided upon. It is, quite the contrary, our *truest* state—and quite attainable in a lifetime. It is actually imperative that one does—or is at least consistently developing in that direction on the *Pathway to Self-Honesty*, because it is very evident when we examine our *models* and the *Awareness Scale* that a "higher state" **correlates** directly with a "higher ability" to not only manage *Self* in *beta-existence*, but ensure the most **optimum** continuation of the *existence of Self*. In the most primitive terms: our *level* of *Self-Honesty* is directly linked to our *level* of survival and thus our ability to manage basic needs as a foundation to succeed at greater personal achievements.

The *Awareness Scale* is concisely drawn out from research and experimental data that would fill many **superfluous** volumes in itself. We have simply selected the most appropriate terms that best reflect each *degree*—although many other "keywords" and "**associations**" undoubtedly may apply. A *Seeker* that has understood the *Emotimeter* will already be familiar with the basic systematic **flow** demonstrated on the *Awareness Scale*—however, the complete scale divulges the "blue-prints" or inner workings of the "*ZU-fluctuation*" that result in various states, and naturally for our purposes, how they are systematically linked together. For example, you will discover with each basic state that further *adding* or *subtracting* even a little bit of *Awareness* will promote movement toward another related state. A *Seeker* should spend some time studying the *Awareness Scale* before continuing.

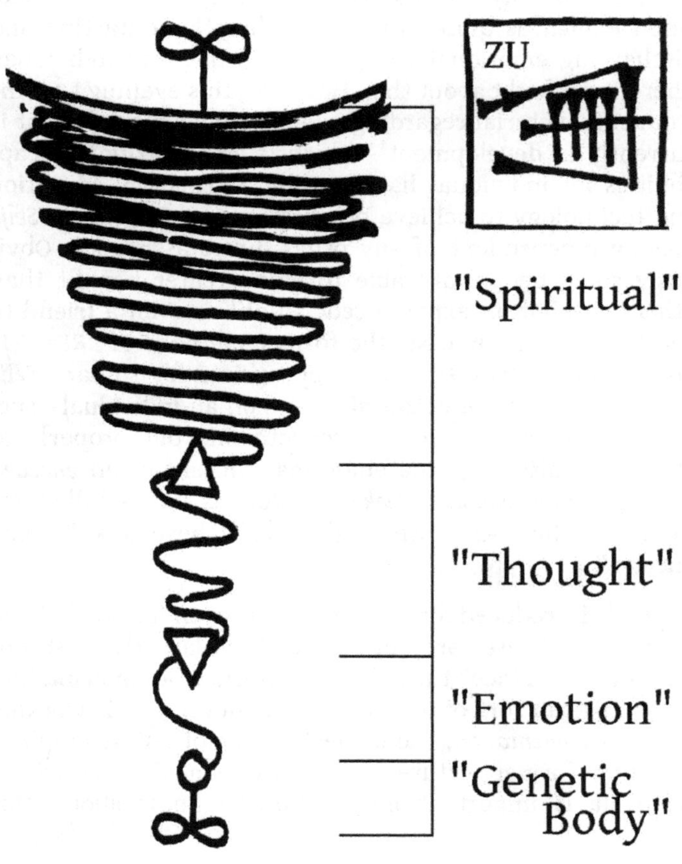

INTRODUCING KENOSTIC PROCESSING

This is a transcript of a lecture given by Joshua Free on the evening of October 18, 2019.

Just over two months ago, I presented some history and a basic formula for ***Cathartic*** *Processing* as "RR-SP-1" at the "*Tablets of Destiny Convocation of Systemology*."* This method, when ***Piloted***, is quite effective in directly contacting and discharging emotional energy wound up in an individual. There is no doubt about that. However, this evening I am introducing material regarding a new "self-help book" that is currently in development‡—which is emphasizing the capabilities an individual has in using *Systemology* education and technology to achieve progress on the *Pathway to Self-Honesty* independent of any other direct assistance. Obviously some people are able to gain greater benefit than others without an experienced "**Pilot**" or even a friend to coach them. In any case, the former methods of "*RR-SP-1*" are not necessarily the most appropriate for solitary *Self-Processing*. Intensive **catharsis** relies on an individual successfully reliving dramatic reenactments out properly to effectively discharge the emotional content of an *encoded imprint*. Otherwise, all a *Seeker* has done is successfully "restimulate" them—and we tend to call those folk "drama queens."

Methods introduced for *Self-Processing*—even if a *Seeker* is assisted in their use—are not intended to blatantly "restimulate" or "**resurface**" the effects or affects of an ***imprint***. But, since this can sort of just *happen* whenever one is working with *defragmentation*, the subject of "emotion" is emphasized in a former lecture series on *emotionally encoded imprints*. It is important information to know about. Our

---

* *Cathartic Processing* lectures given on August 9, 2019; transcripts are included in "*Tablets of Destiny*" by Joshua Free.

‡ "*Crystal Clear*" (*Liber-2B*) by Joshua Free.

attention now is going to turn away from *Catharsis* to another similarly ambiguous ancient spiritual practice that the Greeks called "*Kenosis*," thereby lending to our methods the name "*Kenostic Processing.*" The information relayed this evening will be specifically pertaining to this subject of "Kenosis" and its effective application for our purposes as "*Systemology Process AR-SP-2.*"

The word "*Keno*"—otherwise from the Greek "*Kenos*"—is tied to the old ***Proto-Indo-European*** root: "*ken-*" meaning essentially "empty." This is applied to our ***Processing*** to correctly mean many things—and since each one of them is **semantically** correct, we would have no real need to **codify** or systematize a whole series of "emptyings" or "emptiness" *processes*—but since this *is Systemology* we are talking about, naturally we will end up doing that anyways, right?—in *Self-Honesty*. I mention this in this way because if you start to research what *Kenosis* means outside of *Systemology*, the waters get pretty murky.

The "spiritual emptying" as *Kenosis* has been applied in the past to two directions of travel for *Self* to experience itself in existence—or as an "effect" of its existence; or else *beta-existence.* In Christian mysticism, Jesus *empties out* his "divinity" in order to "become human." The true **identity** of his *Self* would remain unchanged in the Spiritual Universe—as does our own—but according to their definitions, this would be a form of *Kenosis*. We can approach it from the other direction as well—changing states toward the direction of our "**Ascension**" right? If we just keep within the confines of this present example for a moment, we would at some juncture discover that this other *Kenosis* must take place for *Self* to now purge the Human Condition that it once chose to take on in order to return to the Spirit. However, without this high level of *Self-Actualization*, "body death" in and of itself is not any guarantee of actualized "Ascension"—and we are not advocating that as a Route. You'll shed that sucker when you are good and ready. It just so happens, however, when we look back in history that some individuals who do achieve these high states are *ready* *to go* and apparently as a result find themselves becoming iconic **archetypes** of martyrdom and sacrifice.

Methods behind effective *Kenostic Processing* relate to essentially "analytical recall." The better a *Seeker* is able to handle "analytical recall," the more effective any other *Systemology Process* will be toward progressing them on the *Pathway to Self-Honesty*. We are still working within the domain of "subjective processes." Both *Cathartic* and *Kenostic* methods are entirely "subjective" from the point of the "**Mind's Eye**." There are other *Processes* that may be performed that are *objective*, eyes wide open, dealing with the **space** around us—but these tend to be more difficult to manage and direct properly as solitary *Self-Processing*. I do intend to include some in the "self-help book." But, for the moment, I have decided to focus specifically on "analytical recall" for *Self-Processing*. Hence: "AR-SP-2."

Routes of *defragmentation* all involve some measure of "emptying out" whatever is *not* "*Self*." When we are running *Cathartic* or *Kenostic* techniques we are always "emptying out" the emotional **charges** stored within *imprints* or the *thought-formed* "*beliefs*" we feed our energy into. In order to reclaim the energy, the ZU, the *Knowingness*, and the freedom of the *Spirit* that takes up this Human Condition, it is obviously required that we "purge" everything that is not the *Alpha Self*. These are all methods to ultimately return the *Awareness* of the *Seeker* back toward the "spiritual." The only reason there is any sense of "wonder" and "discovery" attached to this is because we have apparently forgotten that we have trod upon this very same *Pathway* at least once before, on our descent into the Human Condition for at least this present lifetime—and however many other countless times our *Spirit* has crossed with the planet Earth.

Why do we call an individual on the *Pathway to Self-Honesty* a "*Seeker*"? It is because that individual has set out to recover something that has been lost or forgotten. Apparently our "sense of *Self*" was misplaced somewhere along the way as we took on these shells. But the very fact that we have descended this *Pathway* before is of tremendous benefit to us in recognizing the truth of our *Self*, the Reality around us and all of Existence. Because it is this inner sense that allows us to recognize it when we achieve it or find it. It is that very recognition—that sense when reading or working through *Systemology* that we somehow *already know* this information and find it strange that it should have taken so long for someone to systematize the knowledge—it is that very recognition that **validates** the Reality of this *Path* for the *Seeker*.

Make no mistake: although *Kenostic Processing* is introduced within the framework of solitary *Self-Processing*, the formula of "AR-SP-2" is a very effective standard ***Pilot*** procedure. In fact, although education and tools for directly ***resurfacing*** *imprints* are necessary to maintain certainty and confidence required for *Piloting* others, these other *Kenostic* methods of "analytical recall" are actually preferred—whether working alone or otherwise. Therefore, it may be stated at this juncture of research and discovery that "AR-SP-2" is the Route preferred when it may be applied; and that "RR-SP-1" is used only when necessary—such as when an *imprint* is stimulated. It may also be the case that an individual has kept *Awareness* so deeply wrapped up in their *imprints* and *conditioning* that the more intensive Route is necessarily taken only to free an individual up enough to actually achieve true *analytical* levels of *Awareness*. It is demonstrated that at the highest levels of *beta-Awareness*, a *Seeker* may effectively demonstrate greater *Self-control* in handling their own *imprints*.

I dispensed some details concerning the "RCC" ***Reactive Control Center*** and "MCC" ***Master Control Center*** in regards to the ZU-line and *Standard Model* for the "*Tablets of Destiny*" book. These centers of energy regulation are at the relative points of (2.0) and (4.0) on the *Awareness Scale*. At the level of "Thought"—ranging between (2.0) and (4.0)—we have various degrees of analytical thought **capable** of being achieved as *beta-Awareness*. This is not a pipe-dream: "Full beta-Awareness" is simply "Full beta-Awareness." That's just about bringing us back up to "zero," right? I mean, how is it that we have come to such a state in the Human Condition that this idea of being "fully present" in *beta* as our *Self* is such an amazingly extraordinary thing to achieve? We won't even try to unravel that with the time allotted to us today; suffice it to say, there is a range of **potential** *Awareness* while occupying the Human Condition, and as soon as our *Awareness* drops to a point of any degree of autonomy—at (2.0) or below—we are already down to only "25%" of our "Full" *beta-Awareness* as *Self.*

Now, I should point out here that our maths on this are not out of whack. Someone asked me about this the other day. If you look at the *Awareness Actualization* percentages for *Beta* range—up to (4.0)—there would seem to be something happening here that doesn't follow normal math logic—but that is only because of another key to understanding the *ZU-line* on the *Standard Model* that has not been sufficiently described until now.

Our understanding and graphic representation of the *ZU-line* is as a waveform or frequency. The vibration type increases as we move "higher"—away from the direction of the Physical Universe (KI) toward the direction of the Spiritual Universe (AN). Just so you know, the entire line represents an expression of *constant energy* between "Infinity and Infinity"—but we are mainly treating the positive scale of **potential** *is-ness* and *Beingness* between physical **continuity** (0.0) and *Infinity*, which is plotted at (8.0) on the *Standard Model* or *ZU-line*. As we move up the scale and increase in frequency, each area or level actually demonstrates more energy in a **space**—more potential—but exceptionally more energy in the same relative space or distance of time.

Further advanced *Systemology* texts will be developed in the future concerning Universes—because this is actually something that *Alpha Spirits* have a causal **responsibility** of creating once actualized—but the idea of frequency and vibration is something that we are dealing with every step of the way. Right now, it is important to mainly understand one key aspect: the energy contained between, for example, the zone or range between (1.0) and (2.0) is far smaller, more finite, lower energy, less **space** in time, slower vibrations—and so forth—than the distance between (2.0) and (3.0); and so on up the *Scale, Chart* or *Model.* There are many ways in which this is directly demonstrable in *beta existence.* For example: an individual operating in a higher state of *Awareness* is able to conduct a greater amount of energy in space within a fixed amount of time—which is why they maintain an increased "reach" or greater sphere of influence (and existence) as a result—and they get more accomplished in the same amount of time. That's all that make's time relative; the frequency.

The light *Kenostic Processing* methods delivered in our "self-help" book are just as effectively performed as *piloted* techniques. Although we are focusing our attention on the "analytical" levels of *Thought-frequency*, this *Tech* is going to contact emotional energy held in low frequency bands on *emotional encoding* and *conditioning* just like *Cathartic Processing*. This new *Tech* is quite effective in doing that—but most importantly it is effective in progressing *Seekers* on the target goal of *Grade-III*, which is to restore the personal ZU-energy vitality or *Awareness* of the Human Condition. These "analytical recall" methods provide a direct increase in conscious *Awareness*, use of the faculties inherent in our *beta-existence*, such as perception or memory recall. These attributes directly affect our demonstration of intelligence, and by this I mean not only "analytical" intelligence but the increased *beta*-perceptiveness that accompanies "emotional intelligence."

A directed use—either solitary or *Piloted*—of "AR-SP-2" should always emphasize the greatest "total recall" of ***facets*** to generate the most complete ***resurfacing*** of energy possible. In most cases, the suggested memories for contact during *Self-Processing* are not meant to directly stimulate deep emotional turbulence. Such happens only as a result of an individual's personal *programming.* If the general idea of taking care of personal possessions or being able to express one's **imagination** to others is restimulating a deep *emotional imprint*, yeah that is going to have to be dealt with —which is why we don't start people onto *this* ("analytical") Route without first providing emotional education, such as became a major focus of our former "RR-SP-1" instruction in "*Tablets of Destiny*."

Systematic *Self-Processing* may be performed with the same effectiveness as experienced *Piloted* processing so long as the *Seeker* is capable of maintaining the same strength, integrity and education level as a successful *Pilot*. This provides one additional reason why we simultaneously conduct these "Extended Courses" aimed primarily at *Pilot Training* for the "*Flight School*," while at the same time we focus on the education, general materials and personal processing directly. It is important for me to point this out as public attention toward our methods increases, because there is one fundamental truth I want to keep in mind as we move forward in *Systemology*:

> A tradition fails when it no longer duplicates the effective results of its originator. I do not wish to see a repeat of history with something carrying such great potential and futurist orientation as Our Cause: *Systemology*.

Increased education not only increases a *Seeker's* understanding of *NexGen Systemology* or even ***Mardukite Zuism***, but it increases the personal effectiveness of *Tech* when applied to *Self* or others. And it is equally important. I have always found it interesting that a person, simply by learning to effectively use the Tech can assist in producing progress for another on the *Pathway* that they, themselves, have perhaps not fully actualized. That's kind of interesting to me. Perhaps it has something to do with the combined *Awareness* of the two people involved. But, since this is the case, it should also mean that we can all work together to more efficiently and expediently raise the *Awareness* of ourselves and each other by simply working together a bit. What a concept! We could, in a relatively short time, theoretically elevate the entire **consciousness** of the planet in this way. We *really* could.

Where we have previously targeted hidden and suppressed energy stores using intensive "*Resurface and Reduce*" methods (RR-SP-1 in Tablets of Destiny), these other light "*Analytical Recall*" methods—that lend themselves perfectly to *Self-Processing*—focus on what we general consider "conscious events" stored in our memory. I will not stand here and tell you that there is not a possibility that these methods will stimulate suppressed memories once the various ***facets*** are brought to full conscious *Awareness*, but as a person increases in their *Awareness*—which we now demonstrate systematically with a **gradient** scale—the ability to effectively manage personal memory and energy stores also increases.

It is only when an individual is brought out of a state of total *Awareness* that their *fragmentation* has any effect on *Self* or its perceptions. It is not the idea of *imprints* or *thought-forms* themselves that is the problem. Without any of these, we would probably not have a universe. But!—are *these* creations of ours, our own? Are they always in our control? Are we unknowingly the effect of our own cause?—or, are we totally *Self-directed*? That—*that!*—is what we are really concerned with. Because otherwise—an *Alpha Spirit* is entirely capable of realizing anything it wants to in existence without becoming imprisoned by it. But that requires freeing a *Spirit's* own actualized ability to do this—of which our **channels** are repeatedly cut off the more we decide to identify with the Physical Universe (KI) and these bodies within it. We must ask ourselves the same questions of these bodies as we do of the *imprints* they store and the *thought-forms* we interact with as a result. Because it's become exceedingly evident, the further we trek down this *Path,* that the bodies we are animating and the universe they exist in—*Alpha-Spirits* once systematized and *thought-formed* into *Being* in the first place. It's important to take moments to look around with each elevated point of *Awareness* once and a while—because you might just learn something more about yourself. We maintain environments as a direct product of ourselves. You want to see what is going on in a person's head?—take a look at how they manage their environment; what they're certain of in their **responsibilities**. *Beta-Awareness-Tests* are practically unforgiving on this one point alone.

Systemology Procedure "AR-SP-2" is intended to raise an individual's general *beta-Awareness* level just as is indicated on the BAT test and evaluations of the same. This automatically generates conditions for a *Seeker* that promote increased certainty in personal *Life-Management*—and at the basic core, isn't that what everyone is here for anyways? Why else do we practice any of the traditions, methodologies or techniques that have been provided out there? Don't be shy—each and every one of you has undoubtedly made an attempt to increase this in your lifetime by some type of "meditation" or "prayer" or "spell" or "affirmation"—a million ways of "autosuggesting" some temporary state that will simply help us better manage our lives—even if only by adding yet another layer of "belief" onto the pile that seems to get us through *just one more* day.

These old methods—sub-standard methods—obviously get to be very cumbersome. I say the word "obviously" because it is clear, at least to myself, that a lot of this is not working for us over here in the **Western** world—or at least not effectively fast enough to provide the real results we need to see. I've never been to Tibet or Asia or China or Japan—I don't know how well the **Eastern** methods are working for them over there, first hand anyway. I don't hear very good things about the state of anywhere on this planet right now, though. All I do know is that over here in Western civilization—it evolved from a **genetic memory** that extends from where Eurasia meets and all across to the Americas over several thousand years; we are playing a different ***Game*** over here. I suppose it might be easy for someone sitting up there in the hillsides, living in their mud-hut, to come tell us: "not to be a slave to our bills, *man*." Well, that's all fine and good, but we aren't going to be successful at playing the

Western Game if we reject it, or try to attack it from the direction of "counter-belief." We don't need a revolt in order to upgrade an evolution to ***Homo Novus***. We have reached such high faculties now as the Human Condition, that a *defragmented* individual has but only the need to *decide* to *be* more than Human.

And that is all we are doing when *piloting* our *Seekers*—is freeing up their ability to decide and for the first time in perhaps thousands of years, returning the power of *clear choice* to the individual.

Basic *defragmentation* techniques explored in *Systemology* are aimed at freeing up the personal energy that is tied up, or wound up, in *imprints* and *thought-forms*—and generally it is only wound up in those which we have lost control of, or responsibility of, and therefore are not being treated as our own. In *Self-Processing* methods, we are using *analytical* faculties to reduce the **erroneously** cemented personal stores of *ZU*. This *ZU* is nothing more or less than the essence of *Life* itself, but we are treating the parts of it we can experience or measure—which for our purposes is *Awareness*.

We introduce the *Standard Model* and *ZU-line* and *Awareness Charts* and *Scales* prior to instructing the techniques of "AR-SP-2" for a good reason: they all provide a means of orientating our concept of *Self* in existence, for which we have few other valid landmarks or benchmarks or signposts on which to evaluate. If you can **imagine** the orientation of *Self* in a space and time without measure, one can imagine just how difficult it might be to chart any definitive "pathway" of movement within it. Seriously—an "I" floating out in the wide open spaces has no concept of direction until it *creates* one, fixes upon one, and then orients all other certainty and knowledge to it. Well, are you beginning to see? If not, you will by the end of this lecture series and its "book."*

Alright—so you need some familiarity with the *Awareness Scale* if you expect to meter your results or really gauge any-

---

* "*Crystal Clear*" by Joshua Free.

thing during a process. When we say to "use a process so long as it is effecting change," we are referring to the *Awareness Scale*—or one of its derivatives—as a gauge. A *Seeker* can expect that when they hit an erroneous solid on the *ZU-line* that they are going to dip down into levels of emotion and fragmented thought in order to first bring memories up to the surface and onto the screen for our analysis. In the former *Cathartic Processing* methods, the deepest emotional turbulence, which is generally nonsensical other than pain and **enforcement**, is simply burned off through repetition, but it is not necessarily brought to a scrutiny up at the analytical levels; it's just being burned off as fuel—fuel to transmute or transform the *imprint* or *belief* into free **flowing** ZU **potential** again. We aren't stripping away anything that is the "true" *Alpha Self*—we are simply shedding these layers of skin that aren't *Self* and which seem to only keep us bound and wrapped in the convolution that is *beta-existence*. The irony is that when you get into higher levels of *Awareness*, none of this stuff that seems confusing and mysterious to the common man is actually complicated. It is only in the face of uncertainty that we find convolution and fragmentation. Such distortions are not even on our radar once we can maintain *Awareness* in the clear light of Truth.

A *Seeker* is only able to experience realizations at their level of *Awareness* or below it. This means that the experiences **resurfaced** directly in "RR-SP-1" are only effectively *analyzed* when a *Seeker* is above the level of which those *imprints* are wound up, fixed or cemented.

For example, a person who is afraid—suspended somewhere around (1.5) on the *Emotimeter* with approximately 15% actualized *beta-Awareness*—is able to easily recall and revisit experiences scaled as "fear" or lower on the *Scale*. But, they won't be able to process anything rationally in the range of Thought above the mechanisms of the "RCC" ***Reactive Control Center*** at (2.0).

Therefore, these processes, although revisiting and resurfacing memories which may bring a person temporarily below this **threshold** while experiencing them, may then be able to carry the energy back up to *Analytical* degrees of *Awareness* and discharge it there using higher vibrational Thought. This is partially what makes "AR-SP-2" a new effective advancement with greater range of application than knowing and using "RR-SP-1" in exclusion with no other considerations. You want to be running something until elated, extroverted and enthusiastic about the future of your lifetime and potentials *in spite* of the memory that such and such has happened. So, you run it through, experience it, analyze every *facet* and then decide if there is anything still worth adding to the files. But it should be analyzed and not simply piled up.

It is important that we *consider* all of our past *considerations* while on the *Pathway to Self-Honesty*. This would be one of the key reasons for the effectiveness of these basic procedures. It is important for us to take these things out and look at them, otherwise we are simply storing them up and carrying them around with us arbitrarily. And they *do* affect us —*especially* when they are hidden away, folded up and put away in our pocket. Yeah—that's a sure way *not* to be rid of something.

It is important to realize that we are on a mission to recover our true **potential**—not add something that wasn't already there. That is a big misconception about mysticism and magic and spirituality. But a truth is attained only on the *Pathway to Self-Honesty,* otherwise we are simply practicing Self-hypnosis and adding another layer of programming without sorting out all that lies beneath. We put considerable energy into telling ourselves that things are not as they are, instead of analyzing the original belief we agreed to in making things as they are. And this is one of the reasons why our personal ZU *Lifeforce* and energy has the appearance of being depleted over time—with age and experience —although the actual *Spirit* or *Self* is no different—*Self* is not changed; meaning that the actual energy of *Life* that was always supplied as a constant, is no different at the end of one's present physical lifetime than at the beginning. Something else has changed—but it is not the energy being *fed into* the system.

Over time and with more accumulation of experience, *emotionally encoded imprints* and libraries worth of *thought-formed beliefs* are as like stacks of important books that we have agreed to, taken responsibility for, even dabbled with a bit—but then never really get around to "owning" the knowledge of for ourselves, so they pile up like walls and barriers to seeing anything more—because you see, we have already agreed to the *Reality* of these stacks once. They aren't going to just *go away* on their own. You can try wishful thinking—most of you probably have already. And if we are going to pretend they aren't there and just let them pile up while maintaining some alternate hypnotic state about it otherwise—well, I tell ya, that's the basis for a *psychosis* right there. Pure and simple.

By bringing the efforts of our past to the surface—including those efforts of others toward us, we are able to bring the *moves* and *counter-moves* of this ***Game*** to a scrutiny. This is the only way we could possibly earn any knowledge or actual information from our experience. Otherwise, experience is a rather *fragmenting* aspect of *Life* with no real use. If its purpose is so that we can learn, than we must be bring it out and learn—thus being *Aware* or increasing our *Awareness* as a result, rather than losing our *Awareness* to personal databases and libraries chock-full of all the *Lifeforce* we have chosen to file away irreverently. Basic *Systemology Processing* and *Self-Processing* is applied to change this. It puts the *Seeker* on a track where they are able to unravel and free up all of the vitality that is already theirs to begin with—just hidden away and forgotten. It is about time that we *remind* people just how beautiful and amazing the true *Alpha Spirit* —the *Self*—really is; how beautiful and amazing *Life* can *really* be.

The procedure outline or formula for basic *Systemology Processing* was released in the book and conference for "*Tablets of Destiny*." Therein, I described a seven-step procedure as defined by a list of ancient Sumerian "cuneiform signs" representing words, concepts or phrases. Those steps described do not *only* apply to "RR-SP-1" exclusively. There is a basic underlying formula at work with that one—very powerful and effective—clearly devised by priests and priestesses of the ancient Temples, which may be applied to further forms of *Piloted Processing*. Obviously we are introducing a **premise** of "AR-SP-2" for purposes of *Self-Processing*, but this method is effective for *Piloted* or solitary use.

Systemology Process "AR-SP-2" may be conducted as a basic two-step process of *Self-Processing* while using the "self-help" book—or the steps may be used to modify the instructions for *Piloting* given as "RR-SP-1" in "*Tablets of Destiny*." If used as a *Piloted* procedure, the two steps from "AR-SP-2" would be effectively replacing the "step three" and "step four" of "RR-SP-1"—meaning that instead of the previous steps aimed directly at "resurfacing and reducing" the *emotionally encoded imprints*, we are replacing with instructions for "analytical recall" in this updated *Tech* known as "AR-SP-2."

The two steps, as defined by Sumerian cuneiform, are:

3. *SI* — "to recall; remember; be conscious of in Mind."
4. *SUG* — "to empty out; to clear; strip away; make naked or bare."

Many former spiritual leaders have referred to *Kenostic* methods as, very literally, an "emptying out." And I am not about to say that this is inaccurate, but when we think of the similarities between *Cathartic* and *Kenostic* methods, both seem to involve a basic "emptying" or "discharge" or "clearing" of some energetic restriction that had once diminished the *Awareness* maintained as *Self*. In order to provide some greater sense of distinction, the *Seeker* should consider the "Analytical Route" to be a systematized process of "releasing the hold" *of-and-from* such and such.

In analytical processing work, there is an emphasis on recall and analysis of ***facets*** even more than the actual *subject* of the **imprinting incidents** and events themselves. It is possible, as always, that in the process of scanning various personal experience that some are going to be more pleasant or unpleasant than others—and it should be understood that the first "response" or "reaction" is a good indicator of this "hold" that needs to be "released." Any type of discomfort or emotional reaction to a *memory* is *fragmentation* showing its face—entirely dependent on some degree of emotional attachment and reinforcement as Reality of whatever it is becoming a *cause* to our *effect*—which should only ever be *Self*. By recalling as many of the *facets* at play in our memory of any event we are releasing the energetic stores that are tying that **superfluous** data up beneath the surface of our conscious memory—and actualized conscious is really the only place that memory serves any analytical function. Therefore there is not even a logical reason to keep energy bound up in *imprints* and *beliefs* that we aren't even making conscious use of, but of which affects us—and we seem to have limited space or resources to maintain these *solids* during a single lifetime in *beta-existence*. Once an organism has accumulated sufficient non-survival *imprinting*, it will begin to die.

As a *Seeker* progresses on the *Pathway to Self-Honesty*, the level of *Self-Actualization* is directly aligned with the degree of certainty maintained concerning *Self* and its causal role in the universe.

> It is when we are at *cause* that we are most *actualized.* It is when we are surrounded by *effect* that our *Awareness* is lowered.

I'm not sure if I can even put that in simpler terms. Effective personal management, such as measured on the BAT test, is a *variant*—it differs from person to person—based on the actualized personal level of *beta-Awareness*: hence the purpose of the test as a basic measure. It's only a guide—or a gauge—used to measure progress while using *Cathartic* and *Kenostic* processes. The *Emotimeter* may be used as a basic guide to ***resurfacing*** and *recalling* energies and being sure that we elevate their energies to the highest degree possible. In doing so, the *Seeker* is systematically reestablishing their basic ***Identity***—which naturally carries an increased *Awareness*, extending up even to *Alpha* levels as you may have guessed.

Effective "*Analytical Recall*" requires identifying and analyzing any *facets* **associated** with recalled events and instances. Only after we are able to bring our *Life*-experience to a scrutiny; analyzing the information; evaluating validity or truth; evaluating the effectiveness or rightness of our beliefs; and everything else that we have accepted or agreed to as Reality—only after all of this can we say with any certainty that we have yielded some kind of knowledge, something real.

> Even if we do, in the end, determine that *Life*-experience accumulated in the Physical Universe *is* actually mostly erroneous, well, then I guess we still have learned something real.

And the recall of events must be firmly rooted in our actual memory as we believe things are or have experienced them —not simply a result of what we are told things are or how things were for us. When we take a good look at our memory that we keep all balled up in a corner—when we take it out and look at it once and for all, we clear out the clutter and find what, if anything, there is to appreciate about the experiences we attach our beta-personalities to so strongly. Because that is what we do. So, let's do everything we can do to clear out the clutter from this world—because its getting pretty murky. So, let's start clearing it all up. And it starts with *Self*. Thank you.

UNDERSTANDING PATTERNS & CYCLES

Although the word receives little usage in modern society, a *paradigm* defines the perspective that is possible of being experienced by the Observer or *Self*. The *paradigm* acts as a baseline or "set" for all the established 'knowledge' that is accumulated in memory, which is recalled or retrieved on a continuous basis in order to make sense of the information and energy "coming in" from the environment to form a *reality experience*.

On the Pathway to Self-Honesty—the course one takes toward their own personal **transhumanist** or metahuman Ascension on a spiritual scale—a significant part of your evolution comes from ability to literally "overcome behaviors," meaning overriding the very programming (***pattern***) of which we are given—either genetically or learned socially. It is this progression of interaction with external energies—our responses and experiences with them—that constitute the lessons and life-cycles that we repeatedly find ourselves in, keeping us where we are.

Until we are able to fully appreciate a specific "lesson" in our path, *cyclic* behaviors and results ensue, and in hindsight, we find ourselves trapped in circles of behavior wherein we follow a program of doing the opposite of what we intend to do; pushing away the very energies and forces that we seek to manifest in our life.

NexGen Systemologists are educated and given processes that allow them to view all of the manifestations, forms and variations of energy as a part of the same continuum or **spectrum** of the physical universe.

Often times, the *cycles* of experience that you find yourself in are a **recursive** spiral that is only fluid in appearance, carrying **consciousness** on a "figure-8" plane or "repeat infinity" of extremes. For example; bouncing between states of "sadness" and "anger" that energetically manifest a continuous state of frustration and anxiety.

At the level of physical behavior, the motivation—the mobilizing initiative of movement and change—comes from an emotional source. This includes the chemical and hormonal physiologic responses of the body that **precede** behavior and observable action.

Over time, and by **validating** only what we already believe we know, personal "*reactive patterns*" form from repetition and later come to manifest outwardly seeming as if they are automatic responses: reactive, not proactive.

The concept of being "reactive" versus "proactive" is related frequently in *NexGen Systemology* material. When we are thinking and acting "proactively," than we are actively creating and manifesting the life we want in stability by focusing on personal strengths and the things we *can* do to have affect on our *reality*. This means we are the "cause." On the contrary, "reactive" ***patterns*** lead to mental and behavioral *cycles* that focus on the limitations that other people offer and emphasis on what we *can't* do. This means we have become the "effect."

The Human Condition is self-validating. People like to believe that they are in control of their own lives—in control of their *thought patterns* and *behavioral cycles*. In actuality, this process is quite autonomous and requires interaction and programming ahead of time to be effectively in control. Split-second brain firing in the moment draws upon stores of memory and response tendencies that are preexisting.

Someone who is in effect a "self-controlled" person is one who has taught themselves to not "react" rashly or make quick "rash" decisions on impulse.

While there is such a thing as "intuition" and being able to sense things outside the normative range of information reception, the type of environmental stimuli and external influence that we regularly encounter in everyday life generally earn "immediate responses" based on programmed knowledge, not true "***gnosis***."

Once you assimilate specific data and **semantics** into your 'baseline' or '*belief system*', you will begin to look for and seemingly 'naturally' observe things in the external environment that continuously validates personal experiences of *reality* that manifest. What we 'process' as experience is all about our "*agreement of reality*." In essence:

What we seek; we find.

While these concepts may seem superficial, they are actually some of the most important issues facing a **sentient** human being operating the Human Condition on the planet earth. This work is primarily the result of years of experimental research and philosophical debate on the problem of why most human behavior is reactive and not creative. This knowledge is critical if you hope to not only comprehend yourself but the people you interact with—and potentially influence.

The basic keys or fundamental steps are as follows:

a.) Understanding human behaviors in general.

b.) Tracing the origins of behavior—external environmental influences and thought patterns.

c.) Naming the "**game**"—attributing the correct semantics in communicating this observation.

d.) Releasing ourselves from this behavior cycle.

INTRODUCING SUBJECTIVE PROCESSING

Self-directed personal management and high-frequency actualization also includes the ability to properly manage what is generally referred to as "*stress.*" Our society simply takes a stand that "stress is bad"—yet this is only because the "normal standard issue Human Condition" is not instructed on any higher coping skills except to "suck it up" and "hold it in" until the weight of the load crushes you down six feet under. This is no way to operate *beta-existence,* when we consider the balance of "forces" spreading in each direction —AN and KI—holding Reality in suspension. Therefore whenever there is a shift-change of any kind in a state or condition, the simple fact that there is "motion" creates a situation of "stress." This is not necessarily "good" *or* "bad"—"except that *thinking* makes it so."*

> Here is the bottom line—a powerful key to further understanding everything we are demonstrating in *Systemology Processing* and concerning our personal management of existence: directed *Awareness*—any focused concentration of *Awareness*—whether subjectively ("internally") *or* **objectively** ("externally") oriented...is ***Communication*** of *Control.*

Therefore every *Self-directed Alpha Thought* or "**command line**" from a *Process* is a communication of "control"—so:

Who is in control of your life?

Who are you accepting commands from?

Who is directing your attention?

Who is demanding that you "listen" to them?

Who is demanding that you "pay attention"?

---

* Quoting Shakespeare—"*Nothing is good or bad except that thinking makes it so.*" (*Hamlet*)

These are answers worth recording in your personal notebook, *Seeker's Journal* or *Flight-log book.*‡ Anyone who makes demands on us does so with intents of "control." We have stepped into an area of *Self-Realization* that now requires looking outward directly at personal interactions with others as *beta-influences:*

> Sources of *imprint* restimulation;
>
> ***Enforcers*** of Reality agreements;
>
> *Programmer-authorities* of information-data; and
>
> Those who actively use *effort* against us.

Consider also those who advance their energies upon you against your will, or those that reject your own advances and communication.

We are in no way placing "blame" in these exercises—and many times these other persons are "acting" with the "best **intentions**" in Mind when they operate their lives, to the capacity that they even are *Self-directed.* This disease of "passing blame" carries swiftly between those sharing the Human Condition. At the heights of *NexGen Systemology*, we primarily are interested in identifying systematic causal relationships contributing to *our decisions* to maintain these *Realities.* We aren't interested in "blame." Passing off "blame" leads to a reduction of personal responsibility as "cause" and thus an admission or agreement—from *Self*—to another source as the power of *our cause* and *actions*, which is actually a *re-action* if not fully *Self-directed.*

> —IDENTIFY persons that you *presently* consider strong *beta-influences* in your immediate environment (home, school, family, work, *&tc.*) or directly concerning your beliefs and past programming in this present lifetime. —*List them below.*
>
> 1.) ‡ ___

‡ Available as "*Systemology: Pathway to Self-Honesty Truth Seeker's Adventure Journal*" from the Systemology Society.

2.) ‡ ___

3.) ‡ ___

4.) ‡ ___

5.) ‡ ___

6.) ‡ ___

7.) ‡ ___

8.) ‡ ___

—EVALUATE your past/present experiences with these persons sufficiently enough to estimate a basic ZU-line association for each, using *Systemology* education and experience with the *Emotimeter* and *Awareness Scale* as your basis. —*List these "numeric values" for each name, on the corresponding space marked* with a "‡" (popularly used in *Systemology* to indicate either the "ZU-line" itself or "Self-directed **Will-Intention** on the ZU-line"). *How much and in what ways do you think these persons affect (and have affected) your beta-personality?*

—RECALL the most commonly used verbal statements spoken by each person in your list, or else their most commonly demonstrated emotional state. IDENTIFY any key words, phrases or descriptions you might find when considering these individuals and their influence on you. EVALUATE this data and assign it a value from the ZU-line (which may or may not be the same as what is assigned in the previous list). —*Record this information below for each.*

1.) ‡ ___

2.) ‡ ___

3.) ‡ ___

4.) ‡ ___

5.) ‡ ___

6.) ‡ ___

7.) ‡ ___

8.) ‡ ___

Putting aside your present *Awareness* of these influences for a moment, take some time now to consider your own *beta-personality* and the answers that you gave on your "BAT" evaluation test. Obviously the test itself is very generalized and meant to gauge a numeric evaluation against an objective standard. Therefore, when you answered the questions, you were merely asked about the intensity of specific ***Self-determined*** values expressed in your lifetime—or the ranking of personal significance in each aspect (category) of *Life Management.*

These are *your* scores based on *your* own decisions and choices. Granted, there are many times when *Self-direction* is fragmented by low-levels of *Awareness*, but as the *Seeker* discovers along the *Pathway*, even these conditions were agreements made by *Self* at some point in "Alpha Thought" *after* receiving some type of fragmentation. We later simply go on reinforcing fragmentation with additional agreements and reasoning based upon the same.

After this current measure of *Self-Processing* since your (last) evaluation, it is appropriate to take a thorough review of *Self* and the statements evaluated on the "BAT" in relation to any personal realizations established at this point in your present cycle (run-through) of *Grade-III* work. Consider it a sort of "mid-term exam" if such a concept of school isn't too **aberrative** for you (and of course, if it is, you might want to "***Process* out**" the ***facets*** from that *fragmentation*). As you perform the following *Analytical Processing*, take notice of any particular *facets* connected with each evaluation, such as emotional reactions, relevant keywords used to describe mental states; also any affirmations of *Self* or "*Self-talk*" routinely made, or even associations often vocalized to others as personal statements (and agreements) about ourselves.

—ANALYZE the present condition of your physical body. *—How do you feel about its condition? What words would you use to describe its condition? What influences your beliefs about it? What influences your intentions in using it? In what ways might it be improved? How might you do that? In what ways have you attempted to improve conditions and were not successful. In what ways have you attempted to improve conditions are were successful? What information of it have you observed from others? What words, phrases or expressions do they use? What information of it have others attempted to enforce on you? What words, phrases or expressions do they use? What parts of it are you most certain of? What are your favorite parts?* *

—ANALYZE the condition of your physical possessions.

—ANALYZE the emotion that you feel most often.

—ANALYZE whether your typical thought-patterns primarily concern the past, present or future.

—ANALYZE how certain you are in your ability to maintain your existence in this lifetime.

—ANALYZE the responsibilities that you have accepted.

—ANALYZE any responsibilities you are shying away from.

—ANALYZE what additional responsibilities you could accept.

—ANALYZE your certainty in communicating/expressing to others about things you know.

—ANALYZE your degree of trust/certainty about your environment.

---

* *Seekers* should consider similar types of questions regarding each line of analysis. Make note of the best or most accurate words and phrases used to describe each part. You should record this information in a *Journal* or *Flight-log*.

—ANALYZE the amount of gossip, hear-say, and falsehoods that regularly appear in your communications/ expressions to others.

—ANALYZE your accuracy retaining or passing along information.

—ANALYZE aspects you are presently blaming yourself for.

—ANALYZE aspects you are presently blaming others for.

—ANALYZE what/who in your environment assists you.

—ANALYZE what/who in your environment threatens you.

—ANALYZE what/who in your environment forces you.

—ANALYZE goals and ideals that motivate your actions.

—ANALYZE your feelings/attitudes regarding others you meet.

—ANALYZE your feelings/attitudes about all Humans.

—ANALYZE your attitudes about all animals and plants.

—ANALYZE your feelings/attitudes about planet Earth.

—ANALYZE your attitudes about the Physical Universe.

—ANALYZE your attitudes about the Spiritual Universe.

—ANALYZE your attitudes about Supreme Infinity.

Compare the data you have collected in this *Self-Analysis* to the previous *evaluations* concerning those considered "influences" in your *Self-direction* as *Self*. The truth is that we carry many goals and ideals that have been imparted to us by others in our external environment—these go on to contribute to our *beta-personality*, which by definition, operates in some degree of *fragmentation* so long as it is retaining significant amounts of **erroneous** programming. The basic operation of the Human Condition—and our communication with others also operating their own *beta-personality* of the Human Condition—is always a "source" of *fragmentation*, but it does not necessarily have to be accepted as a standard condition or agreed to as Reality.

There are energies, efforts and emotions in motion all around us in the Physical Universe—and they may all be effectively managed by *Self* so long as the individual has attained *Actualized Awareness* well above these lower-level frequencies running rampant in our beta interactions.

Self-Evaluation—especially when objectified in comparison to the Standard Model—can be a source of "stress" for some Seekers before they have fully brought into realization the very fact that: none of these attributes of the *beta-personality* is the "I." And we of course know this, right? We have met its truth in every spiritual and religious and mystical philosophy that demonstrates the most basic tenet of the Human Condition: that we are spiritual beings in some way connected to the function of the genetic body as a living organism. However, the "*genetic vehicle*" is not the *Self*—and while the entire methodology of *Systemology Processing* and the *Pathway to Self-Honesty* may, from lower-levels, appear to be some extravagant complicated drawn out process, the truth of the matter is: the Seeker is only left "seeking" for as long as it takes to bring this basic fundamental into a total state of realization—and then actualization. Every Process within our current methodology, and virtually every moderately effective developmental or training technique drawn from six millennium of ***esoterica***, all are intended to do nothing more or less than to bring an Initiate to this point. There are a select few that might have access to some type of "magic switch" that could suddenly return them to this higher state—but for most *Seekers*, the *Pathway* is traveled as a gradual process toward *Self-Actualization*. Fortunately, however, the progress does provides enough surefooted certainty to perpetually encourage a Seeker onward, should they heed the call.

SELF-DIRECTING WILL (INTRODUCING OBJECTIVE PROCESSING)

"*Actualization*" of *Self-Determinism* is defined by the level of very literal "*Self-Control*" that is exercised. A person cannot actually exercised true *Self-directed* control in any "sphere of influence" extending beyond *Self*, if the *Self* itself is not managed properly. We may be able to exercise "dominance" or "**enforcement**" in these other "spheres"—but that results only from intense reinforcement of *emotional* energies, which we have evaluated to occupy lower frequency ranges on the ZU-line.

Emotional energy operates at a range only marginally above vibrations of the Physical Universe (KI)—the level of physical matter and physical energy that composes the very physical organic structure of a *genetic vehicle* or body. This is why *Emotion* is so easily directed and felt between individuals in *beta-existence*—or "communicated"—almost to the same degree as solid matter. And we have all experienced this to be true in our personal interactions with others. It is also rather easy to detect these fluctuations with even the crudest **biofeedback** technology of our current age—a fact that only increases an individual's certainty of *Subjective Processing* if employed in conjunction with it. This is not absolutely necessary for success, but it is an option for *Seeker's* looking to find external technologies that directly validate evaluations of progress on the *Pathway*.

Emotional energy is closely tied to the efforts exerted as actions in *beta-existence*. There is nothing inherently good or bad about it—it is a necessary condition for expressing higher level thought into lower level physical activity, and that is all it is. What we are concerned about in *Processing*, is the degree of personal "control" that is maintained when managing physical activity. This is why it is so important to understand and *defragment* the RCC at this present step on the *Pathway*. Because the energy **channel** is a two-way conduit—meaning information is sent back to *Self* along the same routes once it receives "results" of its efforts (or the efforts of others) to analyze. This information coming in (or input) from the environment (or consequences of action) necessarily passes through our *emotional range* before again reaching *analytical Awareness*. And this fact cannot be overstated to the *Seeker* until it is realized. A close examination of all esoteric texts and practices regarding spirituality or mysticism will reveal unilaterally: "Self-Control of Emotion" is perhaps one of the most fundamental steps on *any* version of the *Pathway*. This is achieved incrementally when working with "SP" *Processes* until it is mastered. Let's try a little practice.

> —IDENTIFY an *object* in your environment that is neutral (harmless) and of which you are primarily indifferent to. [Start with something you have absolutely no attachment to, such as a rock or paperweight. Teachers operating within the "Ancient Mystery School" often used something like a candle or a pebble.]
>
> —LOOK at the *object* with your full attention and *Awareness* and ANALYZE the extent of your indifference and neutrality regarding its condition "*to be.*"
>
> —IMAGINE that the *object* is suddenly the most awesome, useful, positive, valuable "thing" presently assisting your existence. Spend several minutes *realizing* this until your emotional frequency raises up to the highest "elated" degrees of joy and enthusiasm that you can possibly actualize. ANALYZE any additional *facets* directly experienced as a result. [This is *your present* (4.0) on the *Emotimeter*.]
>
> —IMAGINE that the *object* is now suddenly an even more amazing, beautiful, breathtaking, intricate and perfect demonstration of manifestation. Spend several minutes *realizing* this until your elated state has increased into appreciating the *object* as the most **archetypal** piece of art, music and verse all combined

in one. ANALYZE any additional *facets* directly experienced as a result. [This is reflective of *your present* (5.0) on the Total Awareness Scale, which is in the lowest *Alpha sphere*—of Artistic Expression, Creativity and Aesthetic Appreciation—but still milestones above where people are led to evolve in societies built around "material economies" only.]

—IMAGINE that the *object* is suddenly the most trivial, useless, negative, distracting "thing" presently attacking your existence. Spend several minutes *realizing* this until your emotional frequency lowers down back into the range of *Emotion*. The more intensely this *Awareness* is applied, the lower the *degree* that is actualized, including a pass-by of the former feelings of indifference, into feelings of anger, rage, perhaps also even fear if a true *realization* is reached that this *object* is suddenly pure **anathema** to your existence, to which point we will eventually be able to be so low that we are complacently "at one" with the *object*, and are subdued by its control. ANALYZE any additional *facets* directly experienced as a result. [This could potentially demonstrate your present "full curve" or "*Pitfall*" potential from (2.5) down to (0.1) on the *Emotimeter*—although the step is often switched before realized to its entirety.]

PRACTICE shifting your *attitudes* and *emotions* between states as well, making sure before the end of the session to leave yourself in a high-frequency state—though generally indifferent, again, to the *object* itself. The *object* is a focal tool only. YOU can be in control of these states of *Awareness* at will—at any and all times. (And *that* is the goal.) Make certain to end the session at high-frequency *Awareness* after practicing emotional fluctuation.

Although quite basic and innate, the practiced *self-controlled* ability to shift *emotions* and other *states* at ***Will*** by ***Intention*** is something not realized equally by all. It takes practice—as do many of the methods and experiments suggested in *Sys-*

temology—and the logic behind the structure or systematic design of these *Processes* is not always clear at the start, or even always readily **apparent** at this *Grade* of educational materials—but the bottom line is that they yield progressively effective results toward our ultimate goal, and it is for that reason alone that they *are* suggested. Otherwise, the *Seeker* is left with the same intellectually described verbiage as recorded over thousands of years, but which leaves very few true *Self-Honest* avenues to gain accurate realizations. This type of "education" and "practice" has not been readily available or present among the masses for thousands of years—and generally each time that it has **resurfaced**, it has been quickly blotted out or corrupted, or most often reduced to a series of proverbs, morals and dogmas that no longer carry the full extent of the original message.

> FURTHER APPLICATIONS: The previous exercise may be applied several times, as cycles *on* the *same object* and it may be applied to a different *object* during the same session. You may then even use the *two objects* at the same time, choosing one to be the "positive" and one as the "negative" and then alternating the focused attention of your beliefs, feelings, attitudes and **intentions** about each as rapidly (but fully) as you can. To extend this practice further, one would simply select *two of the exact same object* and apply this alternation, but with arbitrary selectivity of one from the other, named uniquely from *Self*, or as "*Paperweight-A*" and "*Paperweight-B.*"

Although we are using this method of *Objective Processing* to draw the *Seeker's* attention toward *Self-Control* of *Emotional* energy—and its notorious slides and swings—the same technique may be applied to lessons illustrating "thought association" (or "associative thought").

This is the basic scheme by which we "separate" things in our Mind-System as being: this *or* that; this *and* that; this *but not* that; and so forth. These "associations" from thought are also linked to our "emotional-effort" systems—they interact with one another and the total result is equally within the domain of total *Self-Control* so long as the *Seeker* is even *Aware* of the "thought patterns" and "emotional cycles" that reoccur.

While it is true that all *things* are not of equal importance, the power that is wound up in "associative programming" that we once agreed to—though perhaps forgotten about and pushed off the screen of present everyday surface thinking—is still "running in the background" of our daily *beta-existence*, of which our "basic" level of understanding will still consistently return to (as an equilibrium). This is one reason why *defragmentation processing* is so significant in all mystical and spiritual schools that have ever contributed to our modern day library of esoteric material.

The fact that emotional energy is carried and communicated by all individuals should not be a surprise. What is interesting, however, is that due to the low-frequency of ZU by which emotions are exhibited, the responsibility for them is rated to similar degrees as *physical* actions. An individual can direct higher-frequency harmonics of "emotional energy" after elevating *Awareness* to the aesthetic range of **WILL** (5.0)—thereby directing expressions of true creativity and imagination. This is a higher level of communication, exceeding the band of *beta-thought.* This is why there is so much "intrigue" tied up in aesthetics and art—and why such aspects are considered "beyond reason and intellect" when compared to "knowledge" in *beta-existence*.

This is where the abilities of *Self* often seem to appear quite "magical"—because instead of remaining solely reactive to our environment, or fixed to programming and *beta-thought* that is communicable in words and language, the *Self*, at the actualized level of **WILL** (5.0) and above, has abilities to *intend* and *Self-direct intention* towards its own emotional manifestation in *beta-existence.* This ZU would normally be channeled into *solidifying Imprints*, but it can also be *Self-directed* to intentionally "**charge**" ourselves, our environment and/ or other objects, with any *beta-energy* at ***Will***.

Although we have used the term now a dozen times for introductory **semantic** convenience, it should be understood that (with the exception of a few examples of physical **enforcement**) no individual can *make* another individual *feel* anything—what we do is communicate our ***Will*** in such a way that *conjures* or *invokes* the "inspiration" for a *feeling* or *emotion.*

An individual must either be in a predisposed state of agreements with a feeling that is now validated, or they are maintaining a low-frequency ZU state that simply puts them in a position to be more suggestible at that moment. Our basic energetic state is always communicated and others are generally able to sense that, even when they are not absolutely certain what the source of that perception really is. However, this can also form into *fragmented imprints* if treated as such over time—whereby a certain person, place or *facet* is now linked to a certain type of experienced effect. This borders on the "psychosomatic"—whereby the unprocessed emotional *Imprinting* we reinforce is able to actually *cause us* to *feel* a certain way due to reactive-response encoding. We can actually make ourselves violently sick and even create disease just to validate our beliefs about the effects that some external presence has over on us as cause. This is a surefire way to diminish personal **WILL.**

The power of **WILL** to *Self-direct* an intended emotional wave of energy in *beta-existence* is a common practice (or **intention**) of nearly all spiritual, mystical, religious, and New Age methods, traditions, techniques, prayers, rituals and creative visualizations. There are far too many names and variations of these to be worthwhile for this present volume —however, suffice it to say that *there is a reason* that initiates, practitioners and congregations around the world, since the **inception** of the current Human civilization, have discovered *any* degree of effectiveness in such methods. The one key feature that is common to them all is: the realization of WILL and actualization of *Intention.*

Emotional energy can be created by WILL (*Intention*) without **succumbing** to the actual low-level *emotional fragmentation* in-and-of itself. As *cause*, WILL intends *effect*. It does not require exciting a personal display of *emotion* to accomplish this either—it may be accomplished solely due to *Alpha Intention*. This is precisely how the "I AM" as *Alpha Spirit* directs all *cause* and ***consciousness*** *activity* form the "ACC" (7.0). Everything above (4.0) on the *Standard Model* and *ZU-line* (and any *Systemology* model, chart or scale) is considered "causal" in terms of *beta-existence*. *Using the power of Intention*, the *Seeker* can simply "*Will*" a desired *effect* to take place "lower" down along the ZU-line. As long as a state or condition is *Self-directed*, created by *Self* and is "owned" as a responsibility of personal power, there is no danger of lasting *fragmentation* in *willing* any variety of activities along the ZU-line. So long as a *Seeker* is fully *Aware* that *imprints* and *beliefs* are their own creations to form and transform—and also recall energy from during *dissolution*—than any constructive uses of WILL are limited solely to one's own **imagination** and creative expression—which are *Alpha* qualities.

The *Seeker* might practice this energetic work using more esoteric methods derived from the ancient mystical schools of philosophy. An initiate was told to take an "ordinary" object, such as a rock/stone, or small piece of metal—some kind of trinket—and "**charge**" it with an "intention." Although there are many ritualistic and dramatic techniques recorded throughout many old dusty volumes regarding this, the basic principle of them all is always the same: *Self-direction* of *Intention* via *Will*. All that is required, is to:

> bring up, conjure, recall or imagine a certain aspect to the fullest extent of "*Alpha Thought*" that you are able—directing the most complete and detailed impression of the "**archetype**" you wish to create and then releasing it toward the object with the fullest extent of *Will-Intention*.

The concept is actually rather simple—however, its mastery was very highly prized among ancient shamans, magicians and wizards, and so a great deal of time and lore is extended toward the various methods and types of practice that accomplishes these *effects*. But, they are nearly all variations of the same basic **premise**, which may be operated on any neutral object in your vicinity as practice.

PART A

—IMAGINE your physical body is enshrouded in a *sphere of light*.

—LOOK around and IDENTIFY a small neutral object you could hold.

—DECIDE that *you will* go and pick up the object; and then *you* do it.

—IMAGINE the object is a **sentient** being that is **capable** of emotion.

—CREATE the emotional feeling of *happiness/joy* and hold it in Mind.

—WILL the emotional feeling of *happiness/joy* into Being.

—INTEND the object to fully experience *happiness/joy*; and then Will it.

—REPEAT the intention and direction of Will several times until *you* are *certain* that the object is experiencing and expressing *happiness/joy*.

—REPEAT the above four steps using the emotional feeling of *sadness/grief*.

—REPEAT the primary steps using the emotional feeling of *ferocity/anger*.

—REPEAT the primary steps completely, alternating emotional feelings fully, making certain that your own emotional state remains independent of emotional fluctuation. Practice repeatedly. (*End session on a neutral emotion, just as at the start.*)

PART B*

—INTEND the object to be *fiercely angry*.

—RESURFACE an emotional feeling of *fear* of the object. ANALYZE any *facets* you associate with this feeling.

—IMAGINE the object is genuinely *afraid* of you.

—RESURFACE an emotional feeling of *anger* toward the object. ANALYZE any *facets* you associate with this feeling.

—INTEND the object to be experiencing *grief-stricken sadness*.

—RESURFACE an emotional feeling of ***sympathy*** for the object. ANALYZE any *facets* you associate with this feeling.

—IMAGINE the object to be *sympathetic* toward you.

—RESURFACE an emotional feeling of *relief* and *interest*. ANALYZE any *facets* you associate with this feeling.

—INTEND the object to be experiencing *happiness* and *joy*.

—RESURFACE an emotional feeling of *happiness* and *joy*. ANALYZE any *facets* you associate with this feeling.

—REPEAT the above steps (of PART B) completely several times until you start to feel that you have greater personal management (*Self-control*) of directed emotional energy and the response-reactions tied to emotional energy from external sources.

Many variations and applications of the above exercises may be derived. The goal of this *Processing* has been achieved (for the present cycle of development) when the *Seeker* has reached a point of personal certainty (knowing) that a Willed *Intention* is carried to action. Ongoing purposes for *objective processing* always involve increasing the *Seeker's* certainty regarding personal abilities to manage *Self-direct-*

---

* Part-B may be practiced as an extension of the previous Part-A session. If practiced as a separate session, use the first four steps from Part-A to properly establish the *Process*.

ion: in this case, the very literal *Will-Intention*, an "emotional equivalent" operated by *Alpha Thought*—"directions" from *Self* that are *Willed* to *beta-Awareness* by *Intention*. And thereafter, the entire **orchestra** of personal interaction ensues from the MCC (at 4.0) all the way down the ZU-line to produce a causal effect in the Physical Universe (KI). When these *effects* are not realized in the Physical Universe (KI) or *beta-existence*, the emotional energy has a tendency to wind up, collect or solidify as an *Imprint-Image*, which later distorts a *Seeker's* clear view of the Physical (1.0) or **continuity** of KI (0.0) from the *Light of Awareness* that is shined down from (7.0) the *Alpha Spirit*—the true position of *Self*.

The full *Self-direction* of WILL (5.0) is rooted in *Self*-control of "*Alpha Thought*" (6.0). Combined, these *Alpha* systems result in the "force" or "pressure" of personal *Intention* that imposes onto *beta-existence* all along down the ZU-line of energetic interaction. In fact, the very definition of "magic" composed by magicians of the early 20th Century was: "to *effect* a *change* in *Reality* in accordance with one's *Will*." As we have demonstrated throughout the cycle of work in the present volume, "effecting a change in Reality" is the very *Game* that the *Alpha Spirit* is always playing with—but getting *others* to *agree* to that Reality; ...now, that is the trick.

To be of the utmost highest **optimum** effectiveness requires WILL to be *Self-directed* with the absolute totality of certainty available as *Self*. The *Alpha Self* is spiritually free at (7.0) "to be" anything and conceive of anything—just as we have a greater range of activity in the beta Mind-System than we do with physical activity. The initial qualities "to be" are only tempered or filtered by other *Alpha Systems* when they are "to be" *Willed* into *beta-existence*. This is in the same basic function of systems that we find concerning *beta-direction* of the MCC and the energy working its way through the range of "thought **channels**" before brought into "physical effect" by "physical effort." This exact same type of sequencing is taking place at *Alpha* levels as well. But initially, a *Seeker* is best equated with a realization of these higher systems by directly relating them to their counterparts as *beta-systems*—hence the emphasis found in the present volume and its former—"*Tablets of Destiny*" materials—on an educational level. *Grade-III Processing* is generally directed toward *beta-fragmentation* and *Imprints* accrued during *this* lifetime—unless something *otherwise* directly resurfaces on its own. *Standard Processing (SP)* Techniques may just as easily apply to these *facets* as well—it simply is not our present focus.

Additional *objective processing* may be easily developed from applications of esoteric energy-work and mystical training passed down to us from the Ancient Mystery School. These initiates would dedicate many years toward a disciplined development of what many today might consider very basic and/or trivial exercises. Yet, some of these very obscure—but simple and workable—methods were found to be highly effective in elevating consciousness when treated over extended periods of personal development. We discovered many of these techniques were first revisited during our modern age most vigorously in Western Europe during the late 1800's—when these ancient methodologies were revived in public sight by "mystical orders," "esoteric philosophy schools" and other exclusive intellectual "societies" that gathered, educated and practiced privately by INITIATION. In America, these same traditions were best realized by an underground—though publicly visible—intellectual movement known as the "New Thought." In many ways, *NexGen Systemology* could be considered a futurist extension of both these previous modern *realizations*, as a means of *actualizing* the best future possible; taking only the best processes from what is even remotely workable from the past for our purposes.

> PART C is a basic demonstration of the axiom that: "All Intentional Acts are Magical Acts" (as stated to us by our esoteric predecessors). This process is similar to *earlier* parts except that the goal is to *realize* a direct communication line of *Will-Intention* between the *Seeker* and the *object*. This includes communication of *Will-Intention* as "control" (using ***command lines***) and

> "**acknowledgment**," regarding the *object* as endowed with **sentient "faculties"** you can contact and *with* **motor functions**. (The *object* is treated as a living being.) The *Seeker* makes a *Self-directed* command of *Will-Intention* to the *object* to the fullest extent imaginable. Then the *Seeker* actually performs the physical action to achieve the desired *effect* and genuinely "thanks" the *object* as to acknowledge the *result.*

In former *Grade I* materials—used, for example, in a "magical school"—an initiate might be given armfuls of fancy tomes relaying all manner of quasi-philosophical rituals and bizarre ceremonial activities to conduct involving this or that type of herb, candle, altar attire and so forth; all of which are *tools* meant to redirect the *Awareness* of *Self* onto the simple fact that everything we do and focus on to the extent of our *Attention* and WILL becomes "magical." And what is that? What is something "magical"? It is imbued with a quality that we have not otherwise been able to pinpoint semantically with *beta-sciences*—and that missing key *is* the matter of *ZU*, and the "attention-units" of *consciousness*, and the power of the Observer, *&tc.*

The most widely used and basic example of PART C is found in many of the "metapsychology-parapsychology-psychic" type research organizations, schools and literature regarding the subject of "telekinesis"—or else the mental command of objects to move. This is not necessarily the purpose of presenting this *objective processing*—but, perhaps at another level, it is not excluded. It may be that such effects are *actualized* completely only after the present Human Condition has fully attained its spiritual evolution into ***Homo Novus***. The reason this is mentioned at all in present context is not to *bait* the *Seeker* further on a *Path* toward evolution, but simply to point out a direct and verifiable fact that these developmental arcane techniques—in all relevant esoteric sources—were found to deliver this same basic methodology to their initiates, for whatever *their* own purposes intended.

There are really only a handful of valid esoteric points to consider regarding "PART C." A *Seeker* should first make certain the object *is* real—the first step of *realization*—which could be a matter of *Self-directed* "Identification" (covered in previous *Processes*). There are also *facets* associated with the *object* as a Reality—meaning anything you may *like* or *dislike* about it. To be effective, a *Seeker* must essentially find it acceptable *to be* that *object*, even if for a moment. So there must be some degree of shared ***affinity*** and *agreement* on the "Reality" shared between *subject* and *object* in order to have valid and effective "communication"—which is any direct transmission, activity or motion of energy, information, data, *&tc*.

All "communication" (interaction) is clear and direct
from its origination as intended with certainty
up to its degree of *fragmentation* at any relay point.

It is important too that a *Seeker* does not get "too caught up" in this exercise. It merely stands out—as do many of the more *objective processes*—because of the physical activity involved and its similarity to other mystical training techniques. It is no more or less significant or important than other practices used to *actualize* and *Self-direct* the WILL—but its greater applications in "other areas" are unmistakable and easy to practice *without* first involving "another individual." The fundamental principle is that an individual is directing WILL with the certainty that the effect will be carried out as intended. Traditionally in *NexGen Systemology*: it is run on a *Seeker* by a *Pilot* to the point where the individual is no longer surprised or exhibiting any reaction that the *object* is not moving (obeying) on its own **motors**.

From the several dozens of examples studied for intellectual validation on PART C, it is interesting to note that nearly all (except some of the most recent publications) seemed to prefer using a *plain clean circular ashtray* as the focal object—preferably one that is not transparent glass. However, in even the cases where it was not an ashtray it was usually some type of "container" that *Will-Intention* could be put "into"—so as to fill it up with an intention or command. All of the example items suggested could also be **charged** with a basic movement (and command) such as "stay there," "stand up," "sit down,"—in the same way we would *direct* any other life form we took responsibility for, but with the fullest extent of our *Will-Intention.* These actions are also easy for us to *affect* when we physically make the change and acknowledge it. By repeatedly doing so, we achieve a greater pattern of certainty in our "surface thoughts" to create change.

The basic methodology presented in this unit of the present volume carries a very real solution when developed appropriately. An individual with difficulties "*recalling*" moments demonstrating successes from efforts in the past will demonstrate greater difficulties later on when expressing *Self-direction* with any certainty. An individual used to being "held back" gets into a pattern that the walls and barriers are there restricting them even when later they are not. These same conditioned patterns may be re-conditioned. In the end, all of these responsibilities for *Self* will fall back onto the *Seeker*—the individual themselves—to manage. You might as well start right now. What you carry is yours to recognize, own and dissolve as you *Will*—but none of it may be ignored if your personal goal is to *reach the top.*

INTRODUCING SYSTEMOLOGY 1-8-Θ

This is a transcript of a lecture given by Joshua Free on the evening of October 31, 2019.

If we look at this chart of *Spheres* and *Circles*—see, originally I wasn't going to even put labels on it—it is the ***Standard Model*** of universes and the personal *ZU-line* that is already given in our material, but which is now examined for "*inter-connectedness.*" Everything *is* connected together as a continuity in KI or an infinity of AN—but between here and there, we *are* individual *Spirits*. I'm not particularly attached to a physical body, but I do like the idea of being an "*individual*" *Self-Actualized* spiritual entity, up here at (7.0)—at "I AM." That's a pretty good place to be. You aren't bound to anything specific—you aren't exactly blurred into the oceans of consciousness like a water-drop in the Infinite Abyss of Nothingness, but you can probably get a *sense* of it from there. Its rather difficult to maintain an *Awareness* for very long up here and then still be tinkering around at lower-levels of the *genetic body* at the same time. But, guess

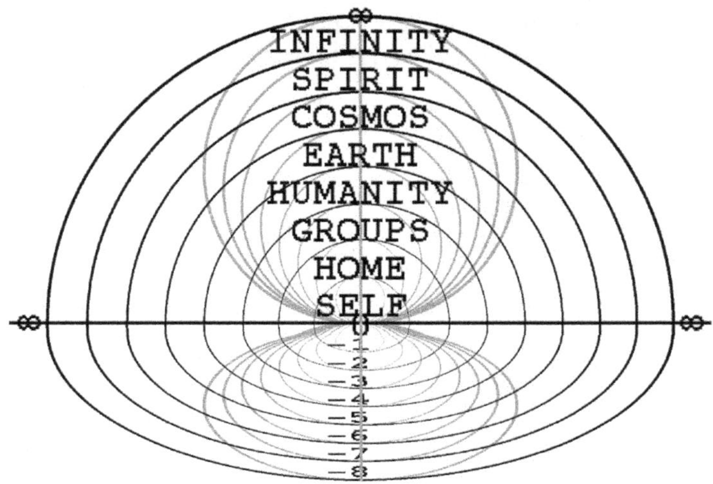

what?—Using these keys alongside *defragmentation* allows for the *realization* of *Beingness*—while still hanging around that physical body you got going on there. Because, you know, these bodies have some use for *playing games*, and that's more or less all we are here to do in *beta-existence*. Just don't forget that you *are* "playing" a "*Game*," because we often forget that point when we enter a lifetime and then get very caught up in this other "My-body-my-self" *Game*.

If you are familiar with the ***Standard Model***, or the *ZU-line* in "***Mardukite Zuism***"—or a clear understanding of the "seven-plus-one model" derived from ancient Babylonian cuneiform tablet literature—than the "*Sphere and Circles Models*" are really more of a visual aid to what you know. But, it is actually more than this. Because what we are wanting to *realize* from this is our ability to *Be*, to project *Awareness* as a *realization* of every point of potential existence between here and *Infinity*. The more we can *realize* our interconnection and influence to these other *Spheres*, the more we gain a certainty of our *Self-directed* ability to *Be* the *Cause*—to literally "*Be Your Own Reason*" to the very limits you are able to conceptualize that, which for most of us, would be next to *Infinity*, once you get that far. This is not some arbitrary exercise—or some fanciful imaginative play without purpose. This also prepares the *Seeker* to start thinking in even higher realms of Alpha Thought related to *Games* and *Universe Logics*. All you really have to do here—and the *Pathway* map lets you off easy on this one—is essentially: "*fake it 'til you make it.*"

So we have the eight *Spheres* and *Circles*—represented in their *Absolute Totality* as positive and negative values for all *space-time energy-matter*. On the subjective scale of *Self*—where we are operating *beta-existence* from the *Awareness* of *Self* and *Self-determinism* as "Cause"—we place *Self* at the center of the *model*. This is equivalent to *Self-Mastery* of the level of *Self* actualized in *beta-existence*—meaning: to the extent that we are able to actualize *Self* in the Physical Universe (KI). This goes back to what we were saying before about the difference between *Self-Honesty* actualized in *beta-existence* and the idea of *Total Self-Actualization*, which is a state actualized exterior to the Physical Universe and "Physical Body," but of which, for example, *Processing* using the data of the *Spheres* and *Circles* as a base, may at least allow *realizations* to the extent of our abilities while in *Beta*. These same *spheres* or zones relate, in part to the *Systemology* we have described, and in part to the old twentieth century New Thought which started tackling these issues over a century ago. But we have come a long way in our understanding since then—or at least our accessible potential for understanding. It must necessarily be that way, because *systems theory* dictates that the complexities of worldly systems will always extend just one point beyond the understanding actualized by its creators—and we are in some pretty deep convoluted bio-waste at this time in human history.

This *chart* then places *Self-existence* in the center at ("1") overlapping the "KI" continuity line of the Physical Universe which is "zero." And you will see that the *spheres* include both a positive and negative aspect to balance the equation. The **sub-zero** ZU-line is dealt with more critically when you are concerned with the creation of *universes*, the *maths* of *logic* and *games*, and the fabrication of **simulacrum** or *beta-bodies* to experience *beta-existence*. Well, right now, you're already in a Physical Universe; its got some *maths*; you're playing a *Game*—probably a few; and you got that ***Identity*** all **anchored** up to the control of this body here. We might as well deal with the conditions we have here on our plate first, and then we can dissolve some of that *fragmentation* with the same steps and learning that earns us higher positions of *Self-Actualization* on the *Pathway*.

The higher the frequencies you truly *realize*—with more than just the intellect and "mental consciousness"—the easier it is to simply dissolve the lower-range energies that are **inhibiting** and *fragmenting* expression of personal management. This is one reason why a good *Processing* regimen is going to alternate between resurfacing and managing an individual's past and present concerns and then focusing on some higher spiritual lessons and exercises to allow for a greater state of *Beingness*—and not simply the *Knowingness*.

I'm sure some of you have spent more of your life dedicated to scoring over dusty old books and stacks upon stacks of "magical **correspondence**" lists and charts then on anything else. It gives a certain boost to one's individuality, for sure. It is all quite interesting and even effectively demonstrates many basic valid **premises** concerning the *Pathway* we are on now—so that we may selectively borrow from it at *Will*. But!—walking backwards nine times around some gravestone while chanting "hockety pockety" between coughs on jasmine incense smoke—yeah, it's a lot of fun and it *is* a considerable step in the *Grade I* materials when an *Initiate* has first begun to *realize* that there is *something* beyond the Physical World. But that is *all* that you can really glean from that work if you are applying *Self-Honesty*. All of the rest of it—you know, the *really valid stuff*—well, we can do those exercises now here in *Systemology* without concerns of getting entrapped into some paradigm of "mumbo-jumbo" or adherence to some distant greatly misunderstood mythological pantheon of *gods* and so forth. The only *spirit* we want to "conjure" is called *Self.* Otherwise, that's not what we are about in *Systemology*. In *Systemology*, we can choose to validate or *obliterate* such mystery *at Will*.

Make no mistakes here about the *Self* at ("1"), which I should add, also includes ("–1"). This is not directly the same as the emotional level of (1.0) on the *ZU-line*, but rather in relation to (1.0) as vibrations of physical energy-matter in action. Therefore, we are concerned with the **existential** *Self* as a physical being and not the "equivalence of (1.0) on the ZU-line. Okay, now, *Self* seems pretty critical in these **logic equations** because if you take that out of this *chart*, then you don't have a *chart.* So, consider *Self* at ("1") as *Awareness* of *Self* and efforts of continued existence *for-and-as* "*Self*" in the Physical Universe. To clarify one last time: This *Self* at ("1") could be actualizing any degree of ZU-energy, like (2.2) or (3.5), whatever, and it will still be right *here* on this chart at ("1") so long as it exists.

The greater we *have* actualized *Self*, the greater our "reach"—and *that* is what we mean by "Spheres of Influence"—or "Circles" if you prefer the two-dimensional approach. So, that means that being statically placed here at ("1"), *Self* remains in place there and all we are doing is extending the *reach* of our *Awareness*, not the **displacement** of *Self*. This is where I lost some people in former workshops, so I am going to explain it this way: think about what you have seen charted as the *Alpha Spirit Self* at (7.0) in former models. Now imagine that instead of moving up into *Infinity*, you are directing that whole scale of personal existence into an alternate reality in the position of ("1"). Your *Self* is still (7.0) in *Alpha* state—the individuated I-AM of the *Spiritual Universe*. It is now projecting its *Awareness* into a *beta-existence* of a specific physical "dimension" in position ("1"). It may raise its level of consciousness in regards to this new *playing field*, but whatever happens to it, whatever it decided to do with direction of *Awareness*, the true "core" or "Eternal Self"—back on this other *Standard Model*—remains at (7.0) unchanged. Therefore, the *Spheres* and *Circles* are specifically related to our *experience* as *Self* in *beta-existence.*

The entire ***Identity*** then—the entirety of a personal ZU-line as *Self*—is manifested in a Physical Universe at ("1"). What it represents is the individual's personal ability of actualized *Self-Realization* and *Self-Control* in terms of personal management, using the total *Self* to form the "*causes*" of any and all *Being*. This isn't fancy word play—we are very seriously dealing with "control" from the point of view of a very powerful force called the *Alpha Spirit;* a *force* that can very effectively direct its *Will-Intention* onto existence. Although many of us have passed off *control* of this *force* to some other *direction*, but this entire *Systemology*—and your personal progression on the *Pathway to Self-Honesty* is dependent on the quality of your own *Self-control.*

When we are talking about *direction* and *Will* and *intention* and—well, we even have all these "*control centers*" in our vocabulary now—it should be very clearly evident that the baseline fundamental behind all of this work is CONTROL and how CONTROL is operated and *who* is doing it. You could probably reduce a definition of the whole field of *Systemology* to this without even using the word "system." When you—or when you *Pilot* your *Seeker* to—direct attention to things, or select things to give attention to, and change your attitudes about things, *all at Will*, mind you; this is all boiling down to "control." Using these methods to control and direct—and allowing you to choose how to control and direct your attention and actions—this is all going to increase a *Seeker's* certainty to *control* personal management of *Self*, and then of course the extent of our *reach* on *control*.

It's not hard to get a realization on *Self*—because, well, *there* you are. So, then we move into the next sphere—and here we create or manifest and maintain some type of *shell* for our *shell*—and we call this ("2") the domain of *Home*, *Family* —basically our domestic security when we flashback to what ol' *Maslow* was trying to say with his "Pyramid of Self-Actualization." Once we realize that we are *Self* "in" or "enshrouding" or "controlling" this body in *beta-existence*, our field of influence immediately manifests toward a condition best suited for perpetuating existence—specifically the ongoing personal continuation of *Self*—and that requires a *Family* or a "domestic" situation of sorts.

Just as *Awareness* of a *beta-Self* "identifies" with a *genetic body* for this *beta-existence*, so too does one easily take on the *Identity* of "family" at ("2") as another *fragmented* level enshrouding *Self*. But, if maintaining full *Self-Determinism* at ("2")—the same analytical efficiency we are achieving for *Self* at ("1")—without *losing* control of our *Awareness* into the second sphere, than it may be used as an effective survival mechanism. I did not drop this *chart-model* on the material earlier because it necessarily requires a *Seeker* to understand the dynamics of, and maintain a full realization of, all the intricacies regarding the *fragmentation* of the *Identity* of *Self* at ("1"), before treating the next closest "Sphere of Influence" as its own "*Identity*" as a "consciousness"—complete with its own associative degrees of *Awareness* and *beta-fragmentation; Imprints; encoding;* all of that.

This idea of *Identifying* with anything other than *Self* from its highest point of independent spiritual *Self-directed* existence is a source of *fragmentation*. Just as you can over-*Identify* and "lose yourself"—as they used to say—at ("2") in the *Family-Home-Domestic* band of influence, well, it obviously doesn't stop there. We move along this *chart* of *existences* rippling out from this epicenter of *Self*, and after *Home* we have the entire domain of *Organizations*, *Societies* and any "identification with a group" out here at ("3"). For any given individual, this is probably composed of a series of various "rings" or "social circles" that may be independent of one another and still overlap in various ways. These are all indicators of a "group mentality" as an *Identity*, which naturally carries its own *Awareness* level—even its own numeric value from the *Emotimeter* and so forth. Basically any way in which we might treat *Self* as an "individual" on the *Pathway to Self-Honesty*, we can equally evaluate one or another of these *Circles* and *Spheres* as an entity. There is no question about that. And it makes for an excellent *Systemology* exercise.

The remaining "Spheres of Influence" correspond to greater and greater circles of inclusion. For example, our *Home* is a basis for *Self* in terms of a "base of operations" for the Physical Universe (KI). It includes others who are in our vicinity or proximity—those within our immediate sphere of close personal influence. This a two-way interaction of influence and control—and it is greatly *fragmented* because most of the *emotional encoding* and *Imprinting* that is deeply rooted during this *Lifetime* comes from "family"—and usually in a direction of "authority of."

All communication in *beta-existence* is aberrative...

...and perhaps the greatest and most intense examples of this will come from our *partners* and "elders" who like to remind us so often how "they know better" and how "you just gotta such and such" and all that.

Your present assignment then is to "*Process-out*" all of the programmed *fragmentation* associated with everything to do with the concept of CONTROL—the literal word; any time its been used as an effort toward you; any time you attempted it and were successful; unsuccessful; anything that shows up in *Processing* that would **inhibit** you from exercising the utmost peak of potential regarding true *Self-Honest "Control."* You can do this with any concept that you want to release programming on.

You're basically working out the agreements and statements made that allowed whatever involved the concept of CONTROL to suddenly be considered "wrong"—much like what contemporary society holds in regards to the concept of RESPONSIBILITY and other key words that represent the power that is inherently yours, but of which has been disguised as "bad." The **fallacy** is disguised quite obscurely:

Don't eat from this tree—lest ye be as gods.

Looking over our *Circles* and *Spheres*: we directly align consistently with our other *models, scales* and such only at ("0"), ("4") and ("8"). So, naturally at ("4") we have the "Sphere of the Human Condition"—or else *Humanity*, the *Homo Sapien* creatures, or *Homo Sapien Sapien* depending on your preference. Our goal in *Systemology* is to elevate the state known as *Homo Sapien* to its next spiritual evolution on the *Pathway to Self-Honesty* as what some are calling "***Homo Novus.***" This is apparently a name that some in the *NexGen Systemology Society (NSS)* are using to officially classify the achieved state of *Self-Honesty*. It is the Sphere of Humanity that we are applying efforts to influence from the sphere of *Systemology-as-Organization* ("3"). The energetic harmonics are presented on this *chart* with its ripple-effects. When *Self-directed* and firm in one's resolve as *Self,* the nature of primary influence **flows** outward from *Self*, rather than receiving or *being—becoming*—effects of turbulent waves. We are playing out this *Game* to essentially try to become the highest level of *Self-Honest Cause* that is possible in this existence. But, this must be *realized* equally for all those within that domain to be an effective evolution—or at least achieve a "**tipping point.**" This is why the states of *continuity-zero*, (4.0)-*beta-actualizat-*

ion and (8.0) *Infinity* are the anchor points by which we generally keep *Systemology* graphic demonstrations consistent.

Beyond the inclusive Sphere of the Human Condition ("4") as a specific species-type of *living genetic beta-organism*, we essentially arrive at the zone of *All-Life* on the planet *Earth*—and that includes all *bodies* or *identities* that possess an *Awareness* of *Self*. This precisely means *All Animals*—but we could extend the precise definition to *All-Cellular Life*, because any form of *Life* existing on the planet with an individuated substance-form or body-structure that has a perspective—or **point-of-view**—from itself would qualify at ("5"). The entire *Earth-planet* is also a living body structure, and there is still some debate among early systemologists as to where it qualifies—either as a self-evident all-encompassing enclosure at ("5") or as one of the many bodies composed of a structure in the entire ***Cosmos*** or *universe* at ("6"). At the level of ("6") we have reached a structure for *All Physical Existences*, followed by *All Spiritual Existences* at ("7"). And then of course, ("8") is *always* the qualities of "Infinity" or the "*Absolute Supreme.*"

When demonstrated or effected outwardly from *Self*, these *Spheres* and *Circles* represent the equivalence of *Mastery*, which is to say "true leadership" in *Self-Honesty*. This is a rare quality in our society today because everyone is bred to be a "follower"—to simply perform tasks of applying our *Efforts* and personal ZU to copying-and-pasting any programming we are given. *Well, who wants to settle for that?!* Look what that mentality is doing to our planet. Do you really think the *Self* in this center spot *here* is even being actualized by the Human population at ("1")? No. *Here*: ("–1"). Not remotely *Self-Actualized*—still primarily a reactive effect of some other cause. Have you met a lot of *really Aware* people out there walking around? And its a slippery slope of "influence" with non-constructive effects spiraling down... and down...and down.

An individual down at ("–1") is now subject to their RCC pretty bad. They may be even worse off than that: with very little or no *Self-Awareness* and just running on reactive-response mechanisms. You will find less *leadership* and *individuality*—more *automation* and *hive-mind*—as you move downward. The individual is becoming the invert of a leader; the invert of causes; the invert of individuality and away from *Identification* with *Self—any "Self."* Rather than exercising *Self-Direction*, such as we see in climbing upward to greater *realizations* of *Beingness*, the defining lines of individuality blur and become too extravagant and overwhelming or overpowering to be managed. So, an individual's sense of *Beingness* diminishes to the same degree as we see it expand in the other direction.

At ("–2") the lack of *individuality* or *Self-identification* leads to a lack of actualized ability or realized certainty to properly manage a domestic situation—and that personality quickly becomes antagonistic to them, including those maintained by others. You find they have a sentiment of "married people are trapped" and "people are better off alone" and all that—that is a ("-2"). Not very *Self-Actualized* individuals make a lot of "generalizations" about "people" because the individual will not see a solution to problems of domestic life, therefore the tendency becomes to exaggerate all of the "negative qualities" that can be attached to close relationships. If it cannot be *realized*, then it has to be *negated* in order to be managed—it has to be *rejected*. This, too, causes a sort of *fragmentation* that will inhibit individuals from reaching or expanding *Self* outward in the other direction to collect together and invite the qualities and resources necessary to establish these conditions.

Those who trudge through the grime of a highly *fragmented* existence and somehow manage to still reach those expressions will most likely self-destruct in view of the fact of any successes, or else sabotage their relationships. Keep in mind, this individual has already accepted and agreed to the programming that "marriage is bad" and that they are "better off alone." Do you see how that works? An individual puts a whole mess of energy into making one kind of understandable and manageable reality with a belief, agreement or **postulate** of some type and then some time later, thinks, "well, I'll just sweep that under the rug," or maybe doesn't even remember making this contract with *Self*, and they just go about things as if these former agreements don't exist. Well, I tell you what, you might even have some programming about "marriage" from your parents or some other authority source that isn't even your own. And if that is not effectively "*Processed-out*" then you can rest assure that this individual is going to carry these beliefs into their marriage, thinking anything can just be resolved with "a little positive thinking." *Nah-ah.*

Its quite possible that by this point you are realizing the value behind this idea of *Imagining* the *Beingness* of each subsequent "Circle of Influence" or "Sphere of Existence" as *Processing*. In performing the basic exercises, manipulating various visualizations or "thought-forms" at *Will*, you are undoubtedly going to be *resurfacing* any significant *emotional encoding* or event-based *imprints* regarding your programming toward any of these points. When you look at the constructive creative positive values on the **spectrum**, an individual is extending a solid reach into the environment; but at sub-levels, an individual is shrinking away and being overcome by other efforts in the environment—and of course, to equal and opposite degrees in the universe.

Practicing higher frequency thought—even in practice as an exercise—increases the flow of personal ZU, the communication of *Clear Light* throughout the *Identity* to the extent of its *realization*. That's pretty profound—yet why shouldn't that be the case? If you can get *fragmented* through some methodical application of focused attention and direction of personal energy—than why shouldn't you be able to get *de-fragmented* that way? All of this information seems so, "Oh, yeah. Of course." And yet, why aren't more people *realizing* a better world out there? Because we can't just place some thin sheet of "positive thinking" over a mountain of old programming and call our state "good." A lot of the more popular, better marketed, flashy, supposed "self-help" methods find very elaborate ways of doing little more than this—which all looks very nice for a minute while the check clears and before the stink comes on leaking through that paper thin napkin you tossed on top.

Now, I don't want to mislead you into thinking that this *Process* of "*Traversing the Spheres*" is a quick routine or some "fast pass" to Self-Honesty *realized* in a single session. Probably not. But the point is to practice. This is what the old mentors were trying to get their initiates to do with the *Kabbalah*—and they called it "*Pathworking*." Some modern revivals of **Mesopotamian** traditions do something similar with the rituals of Babylonian Star-Gate lore, and they call it "*Gatewalking*" or "*Starwalking*." It doesn't really matter what you choose to call this procedure—it is a very old and very useful technique.

As you get a sense or the "feel" about each sphere, you are tracing out a route to it as a thought-form you can interact with—so you work through them **successively** until you can *realize* them faster and more clearly each time: ascending higher and higher. With a little practice, you *could* travel all over the *Spheres* with very little actual effort—and in time, you should be able to essentially achieve any state—and *realize* the full range—of potential *Self-generated facets* in existence between here and *Infinity*. By achieving this effectively, you are essentially opening the internal *Gates* to the entire stores of **potentiality** wound up within and behind all of existence. You are—in effect—increasing all certainty regarding parameters of what is possible. This is *how* we increase the "reach" of *Self*—by increasing the extent of certainty to which there is *something* to reach for.

The divisions, ranges and domains that we describe in *Systemology* are not arbitrary. These **thresholds** and portions are distinguished as critical energetic check-points. For example, to exist within the range of "*beta-Awareness thought*"—what we call, between (2.1) and (4.0) on the *Standard Model* or *ZU-line*—all of that energy must be a certain type, quality or frequency to be **extant** at that level. Sure, it is connected to a continuous continuum of ZU energy as an

Identity, but without this distinction of its energetic transmission, there would be no *scale*, no ***differentiation***, there would be no *universes*, nothing happening for *Self* to experience. It would just be an *Alpha Spirit* or point of *Self-consciousness* existing as itself, standing as *Self*, just outside the *Gates* to an *Abyss of Infinite Nothingness*.

There is undoubtedly a very real point in existence or non-existence—it is directly relayed on the most ancient cuneiform tablet renderings described in the "*Tablets of Destiny*" book—when beta-existences were not yet formed or *imagined* into *Being*—at least before *this* version or dimension of material existence came into *Being* as (KI). These *Arcane Tablets* do not describe this activity as some random collision of forces, but as a *Self-directed* act by a single *Alpha Spirit* with the knowledge and *Will* to make it happen. There is no illusion—there is no suggestion made on these tablets, that the Anunnaki figure *Marduk* is some absolute *First Cause* "Creator" of *existence—no, the tablets do n*ot even attempt to falsely present that as a truth. What they describe is a very *systematic* cosmic ordering, intelligently fabricated from existing *energy* and *matter*—from the potential that *is*. There is absolutely no reason why *realizations* held by the Human Condition should not reach these same heights *right now*.

The following esoteric exercise is derived from the "*Arcane Tablets*" as a practice toward *realization* of merging "*individual consciousness*" with "*Cosmic Consciousness*," which is to say the highest state of being as an Ocean of Infinity (8.0)—written as AB.ZU in *Sumerian* cuneiform.[∞] Even as a practice, such *realization processing* enables the *Seeker* to more easily *realize*—and eventually *actualize*—the highest state of Cosmic Will, as individual potential increases with the unfoldment of *Self-Actualization*. The purpose of such "highest level" exercises in mystical schools and spiritual traditions is not necessarily *to be* the Ocean of Infinity (8.0), but to actualize *Self* (7.0) as a *Total Awareness* of the *Alpha Spirit* "I"

∞ Spoken and transliterated as "AB-ZU" or "*Abzu*"—although actual written tablet renderings use the cuneiform signs ZU+AB for the expression.

amidst a focal center or wave-peak of that Ocean. To fully actualize this from *beta-existence*, one would necessarily have to clear *ZU-channels* of *Awareness* up unto the point of (7.0)—however, the bulk of mystical teachings are found to contain very specific focus-directing creative exercises that often seem trivial at face value but of which actually are demonstrable to achieve effective results when conducted as a continuous regimen of personal practice over time.

—IMAGINE your physical body is enshrouded in a *sphere of light.*

—FOCUS your *Awareness* on the *Eighth Sphere* of *Infinity.*

—IMAGINE the *Infinity* of *Nothingness* extending out "infinitely" on all sides as a great Ocean of Cosmic Consciousness.

—FOCUS your *Awareness* from *Self* as a singular focal point of individuated consciousness in the center of the *Infinite Ocean.*

—SENSE that the *Nothingness-Space* all around you is rising up as tides and wave-actions of invisible motion; its abyssal stillness broken by the singular point that is *You.*

—SENSE that as you press your *Awareness* against the *Nothingness*, there is no resistance, there is no sensation —no feeling of any kind.

—IMAGINE your totality of *Awareness* as the singular focal point of *Infinity*—then REALIZE that the waves you see crashing up against you and rippling into *Infinity* are an extension of your every thought, will and action.

—REALIZE that you are the *Alpha Spirit*; that "wave peak" in an otherwise *Infinity of Nothingness* stretching out within and back off all that was, is and ever WILL.

—REALIZE that your conscious *Awareness* as "I", your direction of WILL as *Alpha Spirit*, and the "central wave peak" born out of *Infinity* are all the same pure individuated ZU—are all *One; None; Infinity.*

—WILL yourself to project *Awareness* ahead of you and see an extension of this ZU as your projection of Identity extending infinitely in front of you—all the way to the *zero-point-continuity* of existence—and back to *Infinity.*

—REPEAT this several times, IMAGINING this ZU as a *Clear Light* radiant extension from *Self*, directed across *Infinity* to *Zero-point* and back to *Infinity*; then REALIZE that you are dissolving and wiping out all *fragmentation* from the channel as you direct the *Clear Light*.

—REPEAT this several times, until you feel confidant in your current results for this cycle of work.

—RECALL the moment you last imagined your physical body enshrouded in a *sphere of light*.

—RECALL the instance you decided to start this present *session*—get a sense of the Intention you *Willed* to begin the session.

—REALIZE that your *beta-Awareness* and the true WILL of the Alpha Spirit are One; End the session.

PERSONAL LIFE-CYCLES

By the laws of observation, any energy or data can be fragmented into as many parts as needed to validate some paradigm. This is why *Truth* is such a philosophical (intellectual) and semantic (communicable) problem for the Human Condition in its attempt for a '*Self-honest*' experience of *reality*. As such, ancient mystics were able to deduce that as it has expanded and evolved at a physical level—or that which is most readily accessible to the sensory perception of the physical *genetic vehicle*—the 'absolute' *All-as-One* energy at the core of existence is present in our realm as part of 'seven rays', 'seven gates', 'seven degrees', but always seven. In regards to other systemological studies, three *cycles* of seven equals 21, and four turns of 21 completes an 84-year *cycle*.

The ancient arts would not be complete if left to simply encompass what, in effect, would apply to hundreds of thousands of people born during a generation. But we choose to look deeper...

While your life-lessons—the *pattern* or order in which you cross specific **thresholds** or gates of realization and awareness—are influenced very strongly by the state/**phase** of the 'world order' and the program 'set' of your generation, we discovered an additional *pattern* that appears much more personal to your specific birth and **chronology** thereafter.

The *Law of Seven* can be applied in many ways. In this instance we evoke two different life-cycles in conjunction to one another. Essentially, we draw from seven *phases*, applying them differently to consider:

Seven-Year *cycle* = 7 *phases* of 1 year each
One-Year *cycle* = 7 *phases* of 52 days each

We could, on a *systemological* level, add knowledge-data imported from other generational studies or from our **trans-**

human lecture series* and make additional observations for the completion of three 7-year *cycles* to be concurrent with the external worldly, cultural and social systems in effect.

To fully understand the *Self* and others carrying the Human Condition, it is critical to always take that step back and see the wide-angle **holistic** '*systematic*' vision of how all parts work together as one in wholeness—one "meta-system."

Basic charting of these *cycles* is begun on the day of your birth or if charting an annual *cycle*, then beginning from your birthday. The annual *cycle* (*364 days*) ends the day before your next birthday, which begins a new *cycle*. Not only can they be used to gauge and predict a certain degree of external influences, such a charting also serves as a guide to 'affluent' or favorable days to plan or execute specific feats.

Although it might seem folly to some individuals to rely on any such *mumbo jumbo* to aid in one's life—the rolling of dice, use of cards, rune stones and other such items having been taken out of the equation here—it is the observation of *patterns* and *cycles* around us, and the natural forces at play in the Universe, that separates those who live in "the **kNow**" from the rest of the herd; those human-animals who carry the stigma of the Human Condition without the tools, means or baseline awareness to rise above their *pattern* programming.

Keeping all of this in mind, a systemology *Seeker* is encouraged to experiment with the key word associations to these phases and see how and if this appears to qualify either the annual or 7-year *cycle* in your own life and/or that of someone that you know well, perhaps a family member.

The following is one of many possible examples from ancient sources, but which has been found to be variably valid.

---

* "*Transhuman Generations*" is part of the title: "*Systemology: The Original Thesis*" by Joshua Free.

YEAR 1 or PHASE ONE (Day 1-52)

- New opportunities
- Breaking forth/Pushing forward
- Career opportunities
- Business connections
- Favors/Loans

YEAR 2 or PHASE TWO (Day 53-104)

- Growth/Development
- Establishing longevity
- Journeys/Travel (short distances)
- Goals (short terms/within the phase)
- **Logistics**/Transportation

YEAR 3 or PHASE THREE (Day 105-156)

- Influx of external energies
- Competition/Obstacles
- Dealings with enemies
- Health improvement
- Relationships

YEAR 4 or PHASE FOUR (Day 157-208)

- Mental/Spiritual development
- New thought/Imagination
- Creativity/Arts, Writing & Music
- Reconnaissance/Info-Gathering
- Loss/Legal issues

YEAR 5 or PHASE FIVE (Day 209-260)

- Personal achievement
- Success
- Goals (long term)
- Court/Law

YEAR 6 or PHASE SIX (Day 261-312)

- Relaxation/Vacation
- Rest/Recovery
- Creativity/Arts, Writing & Music
- Friendships/Social
- Relationships/Intimacy

YEAR 7 or PHASE SEVEN (Day 313-364)

- Loss (aspects of current cycle)
- Evolution into new opportunities
- Change/Transformation
- Testing integrity for advancement
- Completion (of a cycle)

These stages or phases may also be used to represent seven levels of initiation, whereby after a particular *cycle*, the '*test of integrity*' exists to see if one has overcome the challenges of a current level so they can rise to the next, or if they are to fall back into the same *patterns...*

PATTERNS AND PROGRAMMING

Practically *everything* can be 'transformed'. One of the key purposes behind this new philosophy of *NexGen Systemology* is to affect change on a global scale, beginning with the individual, and by doing so be able to shape the NexGen shift in awareness to higher levels as we begin to rise above what it formerly meant to carry the Human Condition. In fact, we are seeking an actualized spiritual evolution of awareness that is maintained as this Human Condition, which in truth, would represent a new evolved species of humanity.

The *patterns* programmed within you—those that affect your attitudes, personality, beliefs and ultimately, your behaviors and experience in the world around you—are all *encoded* on a primitive baseline that is 'motivation'-driven.

Ultimately, all of your attitudes, behaviors, *&tc.*, will be validated as meeting the '**apparent** needs' of the *Self*, or in many cases, the *genetic vehicle* or body that the *Self* controls while it interacts and experiences 'existence' in sensory-ranges of the normative physical world. One of the purposes in pursuing a *NexGen Systemology* education and practice is that it allows one to literally *rewrite* one's own programming!

Future lessons, lectures and volumes of *NexGen Systemology* education will pertain specifically to "programming" and "encoding" and other "*systematics*" of the Human Condition. It is important to discuss these facets now, however, since we are dealing with the subject of *patterns* and *cycles*. The programs that we run in our lives—those that contribute to our personality makeup and attitudes and behaviors that we express—are *patterns*. They are learned and they are reinforced.

The art of "*self-correction*" or "reprogramming" begins with taking personal responsibility for your programming and the operation of your "*Reality Experience*." All of your 'automated' or 'generated' reactive self-response mechanisms may be *processed*, learned, stored or discarded at the 'mental' or 'psychological' level of your identity.

Over time, after applying knowledge to expectations of environment and your interaction with it, these mechanisms are strengthened and reinforced 'emotionally'. That is how *thought* becomes *things* in terms of learned knowledge or programmed learning.

Observers in the field of psychology also note the *pattern*-like nature of thoughts and the *cycles* of behavior, naming the process: *conditioning*. More details regarding emotional conditioning appear elsewhere in *NexGen Systemology* materials, but suffice to say there are two basic forms of *pattern conditioning* that lead to behavioral *cycles*. Both require some type of reinforcement—consequential repetition hardwired into mental associations used to interpret the *Reality Experience*.

In the most correct academic terms, these two types are: *classical* and *operant*. Although these do include elements of "programming" (meaning: the 'mental degree' is invoked through the use of words, data-knowledge and bundles of syntax) most reinforcement is conducted via *encoding*, which bypasses the logical-analytical processing power of the 'mental degree' and goes after the 'emotional'/'emotive' directly. You witness examples of *encoding* most easily when observing the after-effects of '**trauma**' victims. This type of 'conditioning' does not require repetition to be effective assuming the initial degree of emotional stimuli (data-energy) was of a high enough intensity or magnitude and that the resulting condition of receipt was a low-energy level of "victimization."

Classical conditioning is '*associative*'. It filters new experiences based on the *memory* of past results and experiences that may not be one-to-one with 'holistic reality'. They may not apply to the current situation. They may have also not been properly processed at their induction into the 'baseline' knowledge—the "factual knowledge" used to process later data and experience. The same can be said for any kind of *conditioning*, including "operant."

Operant conditioning is '*expectant*'. Rather than yielding to what has become associated over time, this type of programming filters incoming energy and processes it based on *beliefs*, usually beliefs regarding a consequential outcome of a behavior or action.

As we have seen many times in our lives, what we expect as a result of our *beliefs* is not always the case. However, people have died for their *beliefs*, and in spite of logic, reason or further information, some people are so deeply hardwired into their conditioned *beliefs* that they will continue to validate all aspects of their reality experience and adapt it to them.

The fundamental objective of existence is to continue existence, but if we are not learning as we exist, then there is no real growth and the likelihood of this continuation falters. We remain stuck in old *patterns* and *cycles* and live out our lives duplicating the same.

To briefly illustrate "*pattern programming*"—or in our case, 'personal pattern reprogramming'—we might evoke an example from a previous *NexGen Systemology* lecture regarding a concept called: 'Cognitive Restructuring'. There are newer more advanced *processes* now available to the systemologist in practice, but here is the first issue of "behavior modification" that ranks at the height of a preexisting century of psychology—useful only as a basis that we have the ability to "change our mind" and therefore "change our life."

Here, we have a five-step self-checking process of behavioral modification that is entirely self-directed. We can reduce the concept to the following list:

1. Identification
2. Observation
3. Determination
4. Design
5. Examination

First: *Identify* the thought or behavior pattern requiring correction or adjustment. This self-realization must come from within. *Self-Programming*, by definition, is *self-directed*.

Second: *Observe* the thought or behavior pattern requiring correction or adjustment as it is in action. Self-monitor the patterns as they naturally occur. Note any personal emotion or effort applied to the thought or behavior.

Third: *Define* the needs and conditions of adjustment and make a *determination* to follow a self-corrective plan. This may be through some method of *Systemological Processing* provided in future developments or another practical method.

A personally directed corrective program is established only after *identifying* the subject, *observing* its nature and *defining* its causal relationships. Self-correction is self-directed effort to alternate a response when conditions or counter-efforts are encountered. Consider, also, a plan of personal reinforcement.

Observe your personal program in action and measure its effectiveness by monitoring the results. *Evaluate* honestly—then *adapt* as necessary to improve performance.

What we learn is just as important as the fact that we are learning. Nothing is irrelevant from the wide-angle systemological **point-of-view** and there are many minute 'butterfly effects' that yield large life-changing results in each persons lifetime, many of which go unnoticed. The key to the *NexGen Systemological* perspective is just that: perspective—and to keep this clear at all times. Others might say that a better term for it could even be: *awareness*. Being completely aware and unfiltered in your perceptions of the events around you. Judgment, bias, expectations and beliefs —all of this clouds a true and faithful experience of *reality*. Hence, from the point-of-view of the Human Condition, programming and the *patterns* therein is all about reinforced learning. And what is erroneously learned, can be ***processed out*** and unlearned!

THE MEANING OF LIFE

Once learning who *we* are and where *we* come from, the next question becomes: What is the *purpose* driving all life?

? ? ?

When we refer to the '*meaning*' of *Life*, we, of course, mean: *purpose*. And by *purpose*, we mean *function*.

So—have you guessed it yet?

The *purpose* of *life programs* that are *existing* in the *material universe* can be reduced to their most basic *function*:

—To *exist*...

That's it. That's *all* folks. *Life* simply *is*.

"*Life is—existing against all odds.*"

There are *operating systems* necessary for *material existences*; fragmented forms manifested by entities—creations of art, fancy and curiosity—then there are *system-programs* that merely give the illusion of *function*; some-*thing* to do; some-*thing* to give *purpose*. This is actually what many *humans* call 'normal'. This makes sense because it is the state that the *human condition* is 'wired for' and exposed to.

The self-serving *systems* were *created* in propulsion that they might *exist*—and *programs* were written to support *systems* and its *functions*. Everything else that materially *exists* was simply created—manifested—*willed into being* because it *could* be, until the physical universe contained all of the energy and matter in its continuity.

The *programs* are not *tools*—they are not *guideposts*—they are not a *means* to anything other than the *propagation* of the *systems*. And everything not furthering either the *corporeal body* or *alpha spirit* in its ability to survive is a *distraction*—or a game-condition obstacle.

When 'reality' is 'experienced' from the 'mind-of-body'—and not from the 'mind-of-Self'—only unhappiness and uncertainty will follow. When the SELF is entrapped to Reality Experience through the 'mind-of-body', Self-awareness dissolves into total awareness of a mechanistic-body in a mechanistic-universe—but you already know it is more than this...

—So, why settle for less by restricting the conditions of Reality Experience to the body?

When a *human being* continues to experience reality solely as the 'mind-of-body'—or *corporeal awareness*—we say that they are 'stuck'—*fragmented*—into the *I-of-body* and not the *I-of-Self*. When restricted to the *awareness* of a being whose sole purpose is merely to *survive*, no *greater* purpose will be found in *material creation*—a meta-*system* or *suprasystem*—which, itself, *exists* <u>only</u> that it may *exist*.

Until *experience* is *Self-Honest*—until 'existence' is experienced from *SELF*—all of the gathered *experience* will only further upgrade the '*mind-of-body*' and not the SELF. *Self-Honesty* is just a word, or phrase, but what it concerns is the Reality Experience from *SELF*.

Well, what does that even really mean?

Human beings are not as *self-determined* in their lives as they should be. *Self-direction*, by definition, should always come from the **undefiled** "I" of *Self*. When *humans* operate *within-and-as* the *genetic vehicle* they are reduced to *system programming*. The programming becomes the totality of their *awareness*.

Actions become simple *reactions*. What's more—the *action* is already determined by an 'inclination' of what they will choose; a perceived 'choice' to the *Self* and the *mind-of-body* that is enslaved through the *illusion of freewill*. Past programming will dictate tendencies—or patterns of reaction. The fact that you can see in your mind: your SELF—as *body*—reacting to that which has not yet manifest—should tell you *something*.

If you do such a "**thought experiment,**" understand: that isn't just 'playful imagination' you're watching. That's selective-choice programming that you're scanning—what you naturally have selected for reactionary programming *by* inclination; all based on the *system-data* provided to the *body*.

Have you noticed that the <u>*wisest*</u> among you:
—do not *worry*, —do not *expect*, —do not *grieve?*

How could running these *programs* be in *any way* beneficial to the survival existence of the *Self* or *body?*

Philosophers stumbled over the problems of *pre-determination* for thousands of years. The <u>*ILLUSION OF FREEWILL*</u> is alluring!—What they failed to be aware of, was the existence of the SYSTEM.

Programs are written to follow a course to an inevitable end that has been determined. This means *effect* determines *cause!*

It is no wonder that time-programs have to be installed—or the *human being* would realize they are living *backwards. Alpha Free Spirits*—not being restricted to the *awareness* of material existence in *self-honesty*—already know this. It is <u>why</u> they *choose* to *inhabit this one* or *that (body).*

It has been written on very ancient tablets that:

"*No one can see beyond the choice they don't understand.*"

Consider: the initial *choice* the *SELF* makes when integrating with physical manifestation is—in order to experience and exist in the physical universe—is to inhabit a specific *physical body, organic organism* or *genetic vehicle*.

How can anyone truly 'see', 'know', experience, or *Self-Honestly* understand much of *anything* about existence, until they understand *why <u>that</u> happened in the first place?*

BIOCHEMICAL FRAGMENTATION AND IMPRINTING

This is a transcript of a lecture given by Joshua Free on the evening of December 23, 2019.

A basic introduction to the subject of *NexGen Systemology* sufficient enough for independent analysis—at least as it pertains to the *Genetic Vehicle*—would not be complete without examining the nature of *physiological* and *biochemical* qualities regarding personal fragmentation, particularly as it relates to all communications of sensory experience and information concerning the *Physical Universe*. Keep in mind: so long as the *Alpha Spirit* is controlling a *genetic vehicle*, there is always a potential for (what we refer to as) "fragmentation" in *NexGen Systemology*—this semantic of "fragmentation" is quite unique to our *Mardukite* paradigm.

Recent standards providing advancements of exploration into the subject of "fragmentation"—at lower *beta-levels* of personal experience—are explored quite fully in the Tablets of Destiny (*Grade III*) volume; then at slightly higher (more "intellectual") degrees of ZU-line activity within Crystal Clear textbook. Previously, however, I spent two decades exploring these concepts, which I now present so casually using *NexGen* semantics such as "imprinting" and "fragmentation." The **premise** behind these two specific aspects provided much of the original foundation for the paradigm of *NexGen Systemology* as a whole—and in spite of what is already written and presented within our current *NexGen* library (originally distributed exclusively by *Mardukite Truth Seeker Press* and now jointly managed by the *Joshua Free Publishing Imprint*), the concept is actually even far broader than is currently demonstrated at this *Grade*. Case-in-point: I would like to consider a few facets in this chapter-lesson that may influence the nature of "imprints" and "fragmentation," which are otherwise not particularly treated in present (*Grade III*) textbooks. I will provide a bit of background on this first, because all *Seekers* using our material—and certainly any dedicated *Systemologist*—should be quite familiarized with our concepts of "*imprinting*" and "*fragmentation.*"

Whether we are treating a paradigm of semantics based in *Babylonian Star-Gates* or ***Chakras of Eastern*** *Mysticism*—or even some more modern methodology toward *Self-Actualization*—a *Seeker* is given demonstration that there is something "artificial" attached to their *Awareness* as *Self*, and some paradigms go as far as to suggest that these "artificial systems" are even *entities* or *identities* themselves, which are attached to the individual and their experience of existence. These "artificial systems" imposed on the realization of the true and actual *Alpha Self* or *Alpha Spirit* are precisely what we treat as "fragmentation" in *Mardukite Systemology*. So much of the prior (*Grade II*) materials comprising the "*Mardukite Core*"—such as our Complete Anunnaki Bible and information contained in The Sumerian Legacy and Complete Book of Marduk by Nabu*—is already dedicated toward defining "defragmentation" using, or as it pertains to, the ancient *Mardukite Babylonian Star-Gate* paradigm and semantics for a model of this progressive "ascent" or "ascension" up a "ladder" or "*Pathway*" of, what we call, "*defragmentation*"—or else systematic reduction (or processed removal) of *fragmentation* from a system; in this case, systems that apply to-and-as *Self* and its *Identity-continuum*.

Concerning the modern legacy (the Mardukite paradigm) for our present purposes, the subject of *artificial fragmentation* is introduced in the very first discourse of our *NexGen* field; and "*defragmentation*" is actually the title of the second discourse. (Both of these discourses are still available for your view in our small reissued anthology—Systmology: The Original Thesis. All of these original discourses were quite quick reads; very pointedly written; similar to our recently

* All of which are now combined in the Grade-II Master Edition textbook: "*Necronomicon: The Complete Anunnaki Legacy.*"

released booklet *Mardukite Zuism: A Brief Introduction*.) However, I am still going to define these concepts here in this article, because a *Seeker* is immediately lost amidst semantics and *NewSpeak* in our paradigm without it. In fact, the clearest use of these terms and its **premise** is probably found in this original thesis of mine, where on one of the first few pages it states:—

> "The main key—insofar as the Human Condition has the ability to evolve beyond itself or what it's become —is not found in adoption of more 'Systems' or 'layers' of reasoning (and no additional external technologies are required to take this critical leap); rather it is found in the critical ability to systematically remove all of the 'layers' of *Artificial Fragmentation* so that all experiences, stimuli or data can be correctly —*Self-Honestly*—perceived and realized as existence and Reality."

Now, there are some *Seekers* that have not yet moved beyond their misunderstanding of these terms; and hence why it is so important to provide an introductory course that is both broad in its applications to higher points of "understanding" and *Awareness* achieved using *Mardukite Systemology*, but also completely relevant and applicable to the newcomer, in regards to, and demonstrable within, their everyday life as they are presently perceiving it.

To understand our methods and models, one must come to a realization that we are describing a "scale"—a "**gradient** scale"—when we refer to *Self-Honesty* and *Fragmentation*. They are, perhaps, best understood as two ends of an observable **spectrum**, similar to the manner which we might consider "heat temperature." We can use a "thermometer" to effectively gauge the presence of "heat"—or more specifically "ambient heat"—in an area. There is an observable range on this meter and so, at the top of whatever parameter or fixed range we are using—because we know All extends to *Infinity* outside any range that we might plot—we can mark "*Self-Honesty*" at the top and "*Fragmentation*" at the bottom. You could just as easily distinguish other real qualities and mark, for example, the term "*Cause*" at the top and "*Effect*" at the bottom and then superimpose the *Standard Model* or *ZU-line* over this. Such gradient scales are built into all demonstrations of existence and *Self*, using *NexGen Systemology* and the *Standard Model*.

The *Seeker*—or rather their *Actualized ZU* as *Awareness*—is said to be in held in between some degree of "*Fragmentation*" and some degree of "*Self-Honesty*." This state of fluctuation is what provides the elements of "mystery" and "randomness" to experience of *Reality*. Without such fragmented fluctuation, there is no "mystery" or "dark fields" present in our vision of *Awareness*.

For example, you take an optical lens, and you consider that the *True Self* or *Alpha Spirit* at its point of true existence (demonstrated at "7.0" on the *Standard Model Zu-Line*) is using this "scope" to look through the veils to receive communications from *beta-existence* using the *genetic vehicle*; and this perspective is only "true" and "clear" to the point or degree that the field and channel of communication "*defragmented*."

So, metaphorically: if we have a smudge on the lens, then that would be a "fragmentation"; or let us say we are flowing fluids through a pipe or channel that has some obstruction, then that would be a "fragmentation"; or when telephone land-lines used to have a lot of issues with dirty wires, connections and **static** and such; these would all be physical examples of "fragmentation" that disrupts the clear communication of physical energy or power or whatever it may be that is **transmitted** or radiated. Anything of this nature is actually a systematic communication.

Just as I have given many examples of *fragmentation* as it applies to the physio-material universe, there are many many forms of personal *fragmentation* that may carry similarities and certain tendencies—certain patterns that we can even attribute various labels—but the exact nature of *fragmentation* is always specific or unique to the case of an individual.

What we call a "*Seeker*" in *Mardukite* and *NexGen Systemology* is an individual that is working their way through various processes and methods of personal *defragmentation* as a route to achieve, at the very least, the most basic state of *Self-Honesty* attainable in *beta-existence*. This is what the (*Grade III*) textbooks—*Tablets of Destiny* and *Crystal Clear*—are designed for; and what the intended purpose is behind (*Grade IV*) "piloted" assistance.

A basic state of Self-Honesty, once *actualized*—though certainly not the upper-most reach of spiritual ability within our paradigm—but this "basic state" is really what we are expecting as a minimum for our next evolution as ***Homo Novus***. And we have discovered: this starts to have less to do with the biological organism directly and more to do with the WILL of the *Alpha Spirit* that is *Self-directed* along the ZU-line toward the control centers of the *genetic vehicle*. But this WILL as *Self-directed Intention* may only be effected to the degree that the channels are cleared of any fragmentary debris. All of these systems are interconnected on the continuum we refer to as the ZU-line; and any perceived "parts" of these things are just as systematically connected to relay of this information and energy as if there was only one mega-system in operation. Of course, we now know that there are actually multiple systems, working together, systematically, to comprise any conception one might ever have of *The System*—capital "T"; capital "S." Our best stab at such an understanding for this paradigm actually resulted in the *Standard Model* and *ZU-line*. Thus, it *is* possible to *know* real things in this lifetime; assuming of course you are grasping at something *real* to know about.

Elsewhere in our *Grade III* materials, sufficient instruction is provided concerning this one type of *fragmentation* that we call "*Imprints*." For those who are not as familiarized yet with our semantic use of "*Imprinting*," it is defined within any *Version 3* "*NexGen Systemology Glossary*"—which you will find as an "appendix" in any *Grade III* volumes for *Mardukite Systemology*—and it reads:

> "To *Imprint* is to strongly impress, stamp, mark or outline onto a softer 'impressible' substance; or else to mark with pressure onto a surface or **slate**." (And, that's a very traditional definition of the word *Imprint.*) "In *NexGen Systemology*, the term *imprint* is used to indicate permanent Reality impressions marked by frequencies, energies or interactions experienced during periods of emotional distress or antagonism to physical survival (such as pain or unconsciousness), all of which are stored with other reactive-response mechanisms at lower-levels of *Awareness* as opposed to the higher intellectual faculties of the 'Mind-System'; or an *imprint* may also be defined as an **experiential** 'memory-set' that may later resurface as Reality if triggered or restimulated artificially or by one's present environment, of which similar reaction-response systems engaged automatically in response based on an original *Imprint*."

It is not my goal to reiterate or condense several chapters worth of more advanced information into a few moments of this introductory article; suffice to say that we are dealing with a type of fragmentation called "**emotional encoding**" or else "imprinting." This is a different quality of fragmentation than the type that is generally "learned" or "programmed" by more traditional instructional or indoctrinate methods; hence we are not treating "intellectual ideas" in this case, but instead, the type of information that is retained specifically from "emotional imprinting," which we also call "encoding" when the imprinting sticks or holds in place. Therefore, we generally divide the quality of fragmentation into two primary categories: **emotional encoding** and intellectual programming.

Understand: we treat "emotional imprinting" as "encoded" and not "learned" in the conventional sense. Intellectual or mental programming relies on some other type of "logic" to support a communication relay and demonstration of information; whereas encoded imprinting relies on some type of "biochemical" or "emotional" quality for the information to receive substance. The "significance" is not based on intellectual facts, but on *sensation*. In any case, the actual associations of information may or may not be objectively valid or carry truth or be held in general agreement with the Physical Universe; but this *encoded imprinting* will be treated as true for the individual, by the individual themselves. This is really why this is important to know about.

If you want to have a good basic understanding of *Fragmentation* and *Self-Honesty* that is workable, it is simply easiest to treat them as opposites on a spectrum. You have got the idea of *fragmentation;* then you might understand *Self-Honesty* as the completely opposite state—or truest "*Alpha*" state—of clear "Knowingness" and *Self-directed* "Beingness" at the other end of this spectrum. The true ability of *Self* is never less than this perfected state, but *Actualized Awareness* may be dampened or diminished to a point where *Self* no longer has a clear and present handle on its own *Identity*. This is very loosely along the same lines—in *beta-existence*—of when you hear someone use the expression that so-and-so "lost themselves" into something or another, but the truth is that nearly all *Alpha Spirits* operating a *genetic vehicle* for this *beta-existence* are doing so in some or another significant state of *fragmentation*—and of all the types, the information that we consider "imprinted" often poses the most significant energetic turbulence at low-level manifestations of experience. These imprints withhold the circulatory **flow** of *ZU-Awareness* below "2.0" on the Standard Model; which is also below the level of *Awareness* that we would consider "mental" functions.

The fact that *Imprinting* and *Emotional Encoding* is a consideration taking place and given significance "below" the *Awareness*-level of the "Mind-System" or intellect, is the very reason we treat the subject with a degree of importance in *NexGen Systemology*—because the *fragmentation* that takes place at this level cannot simply be "unlearned" in the manner of which "mental programming" might be "unlearned" using *right education*. That is, again, one of the issues regarding this type of *fragmentation:* we are not dealing with learned information, because even erroneous facts, once accumulated, could be dissolved by simply choosing to "*un-learn*" or "*re-form*" or "*re-**postulate***" former handling of intellectual facts.

Imprints may be treated in this manner at higher levels of *Self-Actualization*. Even if there are faulty facts and **fallacious** logic entwined in the programming, such higher level programming can be dissolved very easily with higher-level thought of similar magnitude. But, what about the *Seeker* while they are working up to these slightly higher-level realizations? How does a *Seeker* treat the lower-level *imprinting* that severely fragments and entwines our *Awareness* at the levels even below what we can readily observe as faulty logic? What about the contents of this thing we have called the "RCC"—***Reactive Control Center***—at "2.0" on the *Standard Model*?

Mental programming and intellectual or factual knowledge, even when it is wrong, is able to be treated at the higher range of intellectual **faculties** pertaining to the "*Mind-System*." This information is also stored as a form of "mental imprint" or "mental image" that is quite complete and essentially holographic in nature. It is stored as traditional memory like the film of a camera, and s most accessible for analytical recall. This would be equivalent to what a psychologist refers to as "salient memory" or "surface thought." This is, of course, not the only type of memory that is carried by an individual, but it stores the most accessible programming. The other type—"emotionally encoded imprinting"—reflects an entirely different type of information that actually supersedes higher abilities when viewed from the perspective of the physical body or *genetic vehicle*. We can easily say so, because when examining the ZU-line on the Standard Model, this "lower-level" *fragmentation* operates at frequencies that more closely match, share a higher **affinity** for, or simply are in closer proximity to, the direct physio-biochemical operations of the *genetic vehicle*.

The two main aspects of *beta-fragmentation*—"emotional encoding" and "mental programming"—are interconnected concerning perceptual experience of *beta-existence*, but they are in many ways treated separately for *NexGen Systemology* studies and processing. We generally treat the subject of *emotional fragmentation* first—as described, for example, in The Tablets of Destiny volume—before approaching any higher levels of intellectual processing—such as what a *Seeker* finds introduced in the Crystal Clear course textbook. A *Seeker's* general state of fragmentation is thought to be a combination of both. At the processing level of *Mardukite Systemology Grade III* and *IV*, we are primarily concerned with *encoding* and *programming* most readily accessible from *this* lifetime, although we certainly do no exclude the influence—or "**perturbation**"—of past-life fragmentation, which is treated directly at even higher *Grades*. As should be clear at this juncture, the *Pathway to Self-Honesty* and *Gateways to Infinity* represent a progressive personal journey of increased *Awareness*; specifically an increase of what we refer to as *Actualized Awareness*—that which is defragmented and completely under the control of *Self* as *Alpha Spirit*; the true "*I-AM-Self*."

This present series of introductory articles has placed an emphasis on the more tangible "work-a-day" world applications of *Mardukite* and *NexGen Systemology.* With that in mind: my intention is not to reiterate other readily available materials on the subjects of personal fragmentation, imprinting and defragmentation. In maintaining the spirit of this series, I would like to illustrate some very tangible elements found in personal fragmentation and defragmentation that are not clearly relayed elsewhere—and which directly relate to the treatment of the *genetic vehicle* that has remained our primary focus here. Even if a *Seeker* has not yet studied this subject more deeply in our other materials and texts, it is easy to recognize that the *Human Condition* may be not only conventionally programmed at intellectual levels, but also encoded and imprinted upon using personal processes that very closely resemble what the psychologist calls "conditioning," although the clinical understanding of the same is not actually comparable to our own more widely encompassing holistic paradigm.

Presently we are concerned with aspects of *imprinting* and *fragmentation* directly linked to the physiological and biochemical systems of the living organism or *genetic vehicle.* What I mean is: we are now—at this stage—well aware of the nature of *imprints* and *programming*, the various methods by which memory is stored, *encoded* or even *learned*; however, we have also found that a considerable amount of this stored memory is erroneous, implanted, conditioned and often kept out of direct analytical view.

The *imprinting* that I refer to all pertains directly with "associative memory" that is probably the most subjective type of all possible **experiential** knowledge. "Association Imprinting" forms as a result of *emotional encoding*; it operates well below the treatment of *Self-directed* "thought" and entwines energy on the ZU-line, manifesting at degrees much closer to the lower frequency range of the physical organism or *genetic vehicle* itself. By this, I mean of course, *Imprinting* as tied to emotional **neurotransmitters** and reactive biochemical processes that are "reactive" in nature, and generally are plotted below "2.0" on the ZU-line.

Because this heavy fragmentation is "physiological," "emotional" and otherwise "biochemical" in nature, we find that it tends to respond very quickly to changes in physical environment and other interactions between the *genetic vehicle* and the energies and matter that vibrate at similar frequencies. In brief: our personal experimentation suggests that significant amounts of *imprinting* and *encoded fragmentation* entwined at the "biochemical" range, is also held in place more strongly, kept hidden, or re-stimulated directly, by other interactions within the "biochemical range." For example: drugs, chemicals, toxins, food-additives, and other sources of "chemical fragmentation" may all actually render an individual—outside the state of *Self-Honesty*—far more susceptible to additional *imprinting*; it affects stores or charge quality of *imprinting*; it affects the ability to recognize the "RCC" *chains* and *sequences* directly related to *imprinting*; and it certainly influences the *Awareness* necessary to reduce influences or entwined charges of personal ZU that are withheld from the individual's free use by the *Imprint*.

As you can see, this is certainly some pretty serious stuff that we have stepped into. This should provide something of a preview of what is in store for you as you take up this journey on the *Pathway to Self-Honesty* and beyond, to the *Gateways to Infinity*. But, of course, this journey has a specific starting point, and it starts *here*: making certain that we can maintain full control over the conditions of the physical body or *genetic vehicle* that is presently in use. It should be well understood at this point that while we do very much set our sights on the highest vistas of *Self-Actualization* and a route toward the highest ideal states of the *Human Condition*, such ambitions once *realized*, may only be *actualized* by taking up the path of a workable methodology that will actually yield this result. It requires a bit of work on your part.

The same methods used to *fragment* the *Human Condition*—the same systematic application of directed attentions, focus and conditioning—must all be **processed out** using a like energy and like force and focus. The way out, is the way through—at least if you want to go out the top. As such, we cannot dismiss the *fragmentation* taking place at lower frequencies pertaining to the biological level of the organism. We can select the choicest glass specimens for our telescopic view from *Self*, but if there is a smudge at the other end, then our intention of a clear view is obviously **thwarted**. Its important that we clean up that smudge; because all of the higher level applications of *defragmentation* seem rather ridiculous for us to shoot for with any certainty when the most basic, physical and identifiable sources of personal turbulence are left remaining unattended at the other end.

My intention here is not to **enforce** some personal moral

opinion or ethic on lifestyle choice among the population. However, it remains quite obvious—to those of us looking, anyway—that there *is* a "Way"—or "Right Way"—which promotes a *rise* in personal *Actualized Awareness* and a total return to *Self* as the *Alpha Spirit*; and there are of course "ways" which do not promote such results, and which regardless of the tenacity and repeated effort applied, an individual is left with the task of fitting a square peg through a round hole, all of the while telling themselves they are dealing with octagons or something.

The Physical Universe is designed as such that it does require a little effort—a little work on our part—in order to make the *things "go"* and changes to manifest. And yet many individuals have **succumb** to a belief that the effort and thought, regardless of how it is applied, will somehow be "enough" to carry a clear intention forward; and of course, we know this is not the case. We know that aside from human sentiment, this notion of "it's the thought that counts" or "well, you gave it your best effort" just doesn't seem to pan out in the actual Physical Universe. We also know that individuals caught up in their own "loops"—or "spun-in" on one or another avenue of approach—will just keep on attacking issues "their way" neurotically expecting some other result to take place; one that would actually defy causal or **Cosmic Law** if it were to take place. Of course, the average fragmented individual does not know anything about this; they are expecting some miraculous magical break in the strongly enforced Reality agreements already put forth to carry the existence of this Physical Universe as we are experiencing it presently.

To close this introductory series of articles, I would like to summarize with a concise treatment of the *Human Condition* in relationship to the present state of affairs on planet Earth. (*This is a continuation of the former chapter-lesson introducing "Biochemical Fragmentation."*) It is very important that a *Seeker* fully understands the nature of "*Imprinted Fragmentation*" when these words are used in *Mardukite* and *NexGen Systemology.* This is especially important before considering how strongly these *Imprints* are affected by additional encounters, additional encoding and other facets of *biochemical fragmentation* including drugs, toxins, electronic interference and other types of radiation.

Every individual occupying some attachment with the *Human Condition* has some kind of, or another, assorted *Imprinting* that is based on some type of emotionally encoded experience. This experience has a reactive-response component to it—such as the more primitive "fight-or-flight" reflex action—but actually, any basic behavior response-types may be encoded. The more strongly the emotional stimulation; the stronger the *Imprinting.*

Not all *Imprinting* is "**unconscious**" to us—but it does all contain highly charged emotional content. The more positive pleasurable moments in life do not seem to provide the same intense fragmentation even if they represent irrelevant data. It is mostly our perceived failures, shortcomings and pains of existence that provide us with the conditioned experience and encoding that results in the type of *Imprinting* we speak of at this Grade of *NexGen Systemology.*

For example: an individual might have a negative experience with some kind of "thing" or element in their youth and therefore form a conditioned response to this type of environmental stimulus in the future. This, in and of itself, is actually not any kind of new news regarding the *Human Condition*. However, what we have now discovered regarding *emotionally encoded imprints* is more than basic stimulus-response, as the psychologist might understand it. These holographic imprints are given their personal significance as a result of personal emotion or the emotional **investment** one has with the aspects, elements, or what we call "the facets" of an *Imprint*; and these can far exceed anything that is deemed "logical" or "analytical" concerning an **imprinting incident** and its corresponding reaction.

Whenever an *Imprint* is made, the total quality of the experience is **etched** onto a metaphoric **slate** or frame of film that we carry with us and which may be held up before our view at any time; either on command or by re-stimulation. Contents of any *Imprint* or memory may or may not be valid; but the stronger the emotion, the greater the impression made of the contents. And this impression encodes bits of data concerning all *facets* that are a part of the experience—almost like a snap-shot—including such information as time of day, weather, lighting, moisture in the air, and so forth; not to mention personal sensations, smells, tastes, skin pressures, physical actions; anything that contains some *facet* of the momentary *Imprinted* information.

Any *facet* may be "associated"—or "attached with a significance"—to whatever other sensation or impression is received from the experience. All of this encoded information is treated with the same emotional significance and association below the domain of "analytical thought"—and this is about as close to this thing that some call the "subconscious" that we are probably describing with our *Systemology*—because in *NexGen Systemology*, we actually acknowledge that a combination of all this information forms the literal content of an *Imprint*. (I would strongly suggest studying related materials from the *Grade III* volume *Tablets of Destiny* for additional specifics regarding *Imprints*.)

The purpose for introducing some of these more advanced *Systemology* concepts for this "*Power of Zu*" lecture series is: *Imprinting* and *emotional encoding* may take place *or* be re-stimulated into activity at any time an individual experiences a significant reduction of *Actualized Awareness*. This same quality of fragmentation is even encouraged and reinforced chemically as a byproduct of many "agents" found in common everyday modern living. This is no small matter concerning the state of the *Human Condition*—and it is certainly no small matter when a *Seeker* has determined to take the route of *defragmentation*.

It should be understood that this true and faithful "ZU-knowledge" supersedes any moral imperative that undoubtedly may be attached to our "Right Way of Life" for religio-spiritual purposes and dogma, once an individual discovers it. But that is not our present purpose here; our purpose here lies strictly in what has been found effectively workable in actual practice. It should not be a real surprise that so many main tenets of our philosophy should concur with some or another older formerly known spiritual paradigms. This should only be viewed as a reflection of some unifying truth recognized about existence—which becomes easy to spot once it is recognized. Unfortunately, too many of these former models and methods seem to have fallen short of adequately communicating with the intensity and relevance necessary for present time.

You may find traces of this truth in ancient wisdom teachings, but the exact communication of the former messages do not seem to have been as widely heard throughout the world; certainly not to the same extent as intended by their originator. Or, when they have been heard, it seems as if the words have not been heard correctly.

The present state of the world is my only basis for this judgment and no other specific **demographic** or cultural bias is intended. Whether or not the full nature of the *Human Condition* is already understood by whatever unseen hand directs the systems governing human civilization, it should be clearly stated that the direction we have been guided toward, and the destination that humanity is headed on Earth, is precisely nowhere—or else, nowhere that will sustain the Prime Directive of our existence, which is: *To Exist*. Until such a time that you have *Self-Actualized* the *Alpha Spirit* to a point that you may choose to direct your *Self* to one or another physical alternative form at WILL—even a form that is not necessarily restricted to this planet—(until this time) there is every reason, even ethics aside, to preserve necessary conditions of physical life on Earth, with the utmost respect to the planet as a living organic system and the host of other lifeforms that it supports. The irresponsible enforcement of false power is what led the *Human Condition* toward conditions where it must make a very firm decision right now: to evolve or die.

A true spiritual evolution of the *Human Condition* is what is charted on the *Pathway to Self-Honesty*. The materials that we have developed for *Grade III*—including *Tablets of Destiny* and *Crystal Clear*—provide a solid map that will extend the certainty and reach of the *Human Condition* far and beyond the state it has **succumbed** to. We also now have the much anticipated companion *Truth Seeker's Adventure Journal* available for those working through *Self-Processing* provided in the core textbooks.

These *Grade III* materials are not the "end-all" of everything we hope to aspire to—even within our still developing angle of approach—but *Grade III* is still literally milestones ahead of what has naturally taken place in the present human society happening around us today; meaning both the **Western** and **Eastern** civilizations, for even the distant orient that once prided itself in its spiritual perfection aeons ago has since detoured far from where it once was.

The entire planet Earth requires a healing and rehabilitation of spiritual ability—each and every living organism. It starts with the individual cell; the individual being; and this is where we have started: by strengthening *Actualized Awareness* and personal certainty of the individual.

At this juncture we cannot be absolutely certain where the energy comprising *Imprints* and other personal *fragmentation* is actually stored on a physiological level. Since the emergence of a strong "New Thought" in early 20th century America, many ideas and theories have been put forth ranging from the "cellular level" to "DNA-genetics." It may very well be that the information is mainly stored at a more etheric astral level of existence and that this reel of film attached to our *Identity* is all that we are taking with us from this lifetime.

It may be that we actually take too much with us from this lifetime, and previous ones—all manner of *fragmentation* that still remains to be **processed out**. Of course, such subjects lead us into higher level *Systemological* pursuits—but for our present purposes, we can relay the idea of emotional encoding as interconnected to the physio-biochemical organism and its living systems in this lifetime and even the **genetic memory** it has stored from previous generations of cellular communication at a biological level. These systems —those which relate most closely to the *genetic vehicle*—are primarily chemical in nature.

When we discuss—as in previous articles for this series—the relationship of ZU to the food, water and air that is processed by the living organism, we are very specifically referring to chemical qualities of existence, substances, nutrients and means by which various chemicals are processed by organs composed of other chemicals. There is a certain chemical equilibrium that is sought to maintain **optimum** efficiency, though we know that the living organism is an "open system" and that with the constant reception and expulsion of chemicals, this is actually a continuous ongoing systematic process that is mainly following its own level of the Prime Directive: to maintain existence. There is an ongoing relationship between the *genetic vehicle* following its own encoding for existence and the *direction* and *determination* of the governing *Alpha Spirit*, which independently seeks its own **optimum** means of infinite survival.

There are several hindrances to upholding the Prime Directive ("to exist"), and the first one would obviously be negligence; another would be incidental injury; and then, of course, there is the physical **entropy** that seeks to enforce Cosmic Law of material deterioration of optimum conditions as a defining quality of physical "*time.*" These are the common ways in which most individuals "go out" from this world. Very few individuals actually "Ascend." The condition of "Ascension" is not guaranteed by a body-death. Yes, sure: after this **incarnation**, you would most certainly "leave behind" physical restrictions of your associative-identity with the most recently governed body; but that is no guarantee you will automatically access high levels of clear *Self-Actualization*.

Spiritual experiments for *Systemology* currently being conducted already demonstrate most apparently that *Imprinting*—and the most solidified types of personal fragmentation—are actually more permanent than we originally suspected; even carrying over from one experience of a lifetime to the next and continuing to affect the "capability"—or "capacity for the ability" to direct total *Self-Determined Awareness.* If the highest ideals of "Ascension" were an automatic guarantee—if this were actually the case—there would be no systematic or functional purpose behind repeated lifetimes spent toward achieving this same result; since we can also ascertain that this same lofty goal is applied to an individual's spiritual "Great Work" for every current physical incarnation.

> We cannot even be certain, without a doubt, that the entire experience of the *Human Condition* is not, in itself, an incredibly powerful electronic *Imprint* that has been implanted and enforced on the *Alpha Spirit* for this beta-experience of Reality.

Many of these additional philosophic matters are generally taken up at higher *Grades* of knowledge because they do not, in any way, change the more immediate tasks at hand for the *Seeker* to necessarily achieve their initial sure footing to start unfolding a personal journey on the *Pathway to Self-Honesty*.

It is quite simply in the greatest interest of the individual—the *Seeker*—and of benefit to all those they interact with as a *Reality Experience* in the Physical Universe, to attain (and maintain) the highest ideal state for the *Human Condition* possible during this lifetime. It is no exaggeration that the course taken—the ***fate***—of the entire **successive** evolution of the *Human Condition* may very well rely on what you are doing right here and right now and what you are able to manifest for the future. Systemology provides you with the effective power of ten-million butterfly sneezes. There are very few things that can hinder the incredible potential waiting to unfold for a *Seeker*; but *fragmentation* is certainly one of them—and too often it goes unchecked while sights are set on some higher plane.

The natural biochemical organic processes of the *genetic vehicle*—which maintain its optimum function and health, coinciding with the clearest circulation of ZU energy—may be easily upset by many different sources of personal turbulence; most of which are simply taken for granted by individuals that have grown accustomed to the "modern way" of things without raising them to a scrutiny. There are many substances that can affect the processing and chemical equilibrium of the *genetic vehicle* that are inherent in the "modern way" of life: chemicals (natural and synthetic); drugs (again, natural or synthetic); dietary supplements (food additives and preservatives); toxic hazards (pesticides, industrial chemicals, solvents and waste products); radiation (atomic, electromagnetic and even emotional); and just about every other application of external and mechanical technologies—from automobiles, to X-ray machines, to atomic fission and nuclear bombs. There are literally no shortages of avenues leading toward—or directly reinforcing—one type or another of personal *fragmentation*, and yet until only relatively recently in human history, there have been only shortages in surefire ways to properly manage and alter this convoluted universe composed of agreements so arcane and archaic that we can hardly even trace their origins; we simply adopt them and enforce our children to also agree.

Obviously many aspects of "modern" living are taken for granted; once **postulated** and set in motion by someone in the long distant past and then left to run, or fed continuously to keep running, simply to maintain its place of holding up a delicate house-of-cards that represents the governing systems of the *Human Condition.* Any aspect of "modern" living that is contributory to *fragmentation*, including *chemical fragmentation*—meaning that it affects *Self-determined* physio-biochemical functions of the *genetic vehicle*—should be taken into account while a *Seeker* charts the course of their personal journey toward *Self-Honesty*. It is the same basic *Pathway* for all of us, but each individual will find their own unique *facets* of poorly associated knowledge to work out—or "**process out**"—during this lifetime on their ascent. Such *defragmentation* is a necessary condition of the ascent.

Poorly associated information often leads to setting up automated reactive-responses to the Physical Universe in the absence of true knowledge. The systematic reduction and elimination of this erroneous *encoding* is what defines *defragmentation* and a "way out" from trappings and limitations, which we have all at one time or another agreed to; and with each of these agreements, agreed to a reduced condition of personal *Self-determinism*. Repair of *Self-Determinism* is quite possible using the proper *processing* and rehabilitation of the control by the *Self* as *Alpha Spirit*; but a *Seeker* should be very certain that they are not working against themselves—and their true efforts toward achieving these goals—by continuing behavioral tendencies or contact with **counter-productive** counter-efforts that may hinder—or even render useless and null—the potential gains and wins of our various methods.

When you line up all of the truly effective "spirito-mystica-metaphysical" procedures that appear throughout the last 6,000 years of recorded history—and there are not very many effective and workable methods of note—each one carries and shares a particular commonality of practices or regimens with one another, which may be simply reduced to the most fundamental concept: PURIFICATION.

Regardless of which spiritual source from our past we might turn to for inspiration in, for example, developing the modern *NexGen Systemology* paradigm, we were **confronted** by one version or another of "*self-purification*" rites and formulas. These demonstrations are as commonly shared—across the boards—as the theme of INITIATION, which is defined at the very end of the <u>Crystal Clear</u> textbook. But the mystic rites and esoteric rules of *purification* actually precede the steps of *Initiation*. An "Initiate" is always to present themselves for "initiation ceremonies" only after a period dedicated to personal *purification.* Of course, in *NexGen Systemology*, we treat the truth of these aspects without necessarily **participating** or conjuring up one or another brand of "traditional esoterica"—such as might be explored more thoroughly within its own playing field (in *Grade I*), where I previously provided necessary instruction instruction in these related matters throughout such volume titles as: The Sorcerer's Handbook and The Druid's Handbook and The Vampyre's Handbook and The Elvenomicon and so forth.*

By comparison, the work of *Grade III* in no way contradicts these former paradigms; but we are, in *Mardukite* and *NexGen Systemology*, treating a unification of any such former understandings at a higher order of reasoning—and with an appropriate semantic paradigm that is not restricted to any one or another of these former paradigms. Our goal—my goal—in the development of *Systemology* was (*and is*) the highest **echelon** of understanding possible outside of any one or another paradigm; and should any of this somehow validate something else directly that may be now recognized from back down the **timeline**, well... *great!* But, understand that this is not in any way what my direct intention is regarding this new *NexGen* understanding of the universe.

Whether using some version of obscure medieval sorcery out of an old archaic dusty grimoire, or perhaps attempting to contact your *Self* in some round-about convoluted way as described by wizards like Abramelin; whom after six months of "pious living" and purification treatments would then make contact with *Self* as some external identity commonly referred to as the "Holy Guardian Angel" in some ceremonial magic traditions, or the "Higher Genius" and so forth—they have a lot of names for this thing called *Self*—and perhaps this premise is even set forth with an ancient foreknowledge that there are multiple "entities" interact

---

* Grade-I is available in two Master Edition textbooks by Joshua Free: "*The Great Magickal Arcanum*" and "*Merlyn's Complete Book of Druidism.*"

ing, or influencing, what is experienced as the Identity as-for-and-by *Self*. But, the point to keep in mind here is: even this arcane experimental sorcerer type still carefully observed purification periods before even bothering to apply ritualized efforts to explore new vistas—or open up new gateways of understanding.

Checks and balances at work in the universe. The more clearly observant and *Aware* the *Seeker* is about these basic Laws governing the **Cosmos**—referred to on the arcane tablets as "*cosmic ordering*" as the *Awareness* of *Self* observes the moves and turns taking place in *this* realization of the Physical Universe—the more "amazing" or "magical" the individual appears to be for those who have not yet attained this same level of *Actualized Awareness*; because they are radiate an understanding and certainty of a higher order of reason. Even though they may share proximity—in a similar physical space—with another individual, they are operating their own understanding in all of their activities in a way that is far and above the baseline standard issue programmed one-foot-in-front-of-the-other robotic method that most people have simply become accustomed to getting through their daily existence with; and by **succumbing** to the perceived least-effort comfort-ability of that, they proceed to arrange a robotic determinism of one-foot-in-front-of-the-other right into a grave without *knowing* anything substantial that may be useful for arranging the next level of *beingness*.

When one examines the regimens of monks and shamans: we find equal significance given to the health and strength of the physical body or *genetic vehicle*—and its *purification*—as we find given to treatments of the spiritual and astral levels of existence, which compose the more colorful esoteric and mystical lore that survives in the "New Age" today. To *detoxify*, they suggest a regimen of light exercise (walking or jogging) to increase circulatory flow followed by the use of a "sweat-lodge" or *sauna* to literally purge the body of its *chemical fragmentation*. Fluids, minerals and vitamin-nutrients are also supplemented to regulate and stabilize personal chemistry of the *genetic vehicle* during the process.

Many individuals—when left unaided—often do not change "their ways" because of the sensation of "withdrawal" that often occurs. And many modern practitioners and spiritualists and "New Agers" of every flavor, have too often overlooked the benefits gained from "pious lifestyles" maintained by those we have admired in the past, which have tread this *Pathway* before us, that have achieved—or at least demonstrated some degree of achievement—of true Ascension.

Too often, this idea of "positive thinking" or "creative visualization" or a few minutes spent in front of the mirror chanting "axioms" and "affirmations" is not enough to override lifetimes of bombardment—or even the interference **prevalent** in a single lifetime in the "modern" world. The *Human Condition* requires a bit more assistance now to grant the certainty necessary to rise up and **confront** the sources of turbulence—thereby preventing further (additional) fragmentation.

The primitive magics of any era have only partially resolved the problems by providing a momentary glimpse of something more—something greater than—but too often the individual gets to "thinking" again and snaps their *Awareness* right back to where they were. My goal is to provide a solid route of certainty that will permit any individual living today or tomorrow—or whenever they show up in their cells here—the means, tackle and gear to make their way back out; through and out. What we have actually accomplished with *Grade III* is not necessarily the final leg of the journey that goes all the way out, but our research has demonstrated that those working successfully within this *Grade* are, at the very least, not getting any worse; and they are seeing real progress forward. And as they are able to radiate a more vibrant personal ZU frequency into their physical existence, it is becoming noticeable to those around them that something has changed—and they find out that they are more able to handle and manage the confusions and fragmentation of the world because their attention is fixed on a very real point with certainty—a greater certainty than what they worldly domains have to offer; and that point is nowhere confined to this Physical Universe.

We have discovered that the more an individual is persuaded to concern ourselves with the turbulent confusion of the world-at-large head on—outside of a state of *Self-Honesty* —the more likely they are to be wrapped up in it; to be *of* it, and not just play at the games *within* it. This is when an individual is likely to lose their own *Self-determinism* and **participate** with a series of agreements that keep shifting the **postulates** around to base our *Reality*, concerning, for example, what does or does not make us sick; then on the other side, what makes us well and sane. We are asked to flip-flop our beliefs regarding the medicines and poisons of life—and I can assure you that rather than take the stand of advisement in contrary to some FDA or other health regulation, I can tell you that these suggestions and minimums and supposed regulations are not severe enough.

Existing regulations presently in place now mainly serve business interests and perhaps provide only a marginal modicum of environmental damage control; because of course, if things were on a decline too obviously, then certainly someone would notice—someone would notice and take the responsibility to change things. We would expect. We would hope. Ah, but *hope* is one of the last points before *Awareness* drops out and we are no longer cause; because when we are lingering around in *hope*, we are waiting as an effect—the responsibility now **displaced** elsewhere.

Interestingly, we have known certain things for a long time —certain things about our planet and about our activities— and again, we are not about to make a specific appeal to your political side with our philosophy. There is no political matter involved here. It is a matter of *Life* and *Livingness.* It does not matter what side you wish to take on a political regard, because we all know that the dramatics and entertainment behind social politics is just another fabrication of someone's imagination that has been left to run on its own now—the responsibility for that long passed into the shadows when there was actually a "Divine Right to Rule" in place.

The real agenda is hardly covert, hidden or a conspiracy; when one can determine it quite clearly with a *Self-Honest* examination of what is happening around us every day. It is worthless if I am to stand here and point the things all out to you. That's not interesting to me and it feels too much like indoctrination for you. Therefore, it is abundantly clear to me that we can best apply efforts toward increase of ability for the *Human Condition* to operate in *Self-Honesty* and see things as they really are without the installation of dogma; which is a far more important loftier goal than me just telling you how things really are.

Unveiling this personal mystery is something a *Seeker* discovers when using *processing* techniques of *Systemology*. There are many exercises and procedures that we conduct that do not seem to have any real value to them until a person actually *does* come to those *realizations* for themselves in the process. There is far greater value in receiving truth via these ***gnostic*** channels of pure cognition as opposed to my kicking this spiritual movement off with a large book of dry academic postulates and lists of facts about how things are in the universes. *Systemology* is, and will always be, a route of *Self-knowledge*, which can only be determined as true to the extent that is found effective by *Self*.

The final subject I wish to touch upon for this series concerns a return to a world problem that has plagued us since the end of the second World War—and yet too often now is either misunderstood or ignored entirely. RADIATION. We are literally surrounded by it everyday. There is even a background radiation present, back of the entire Physical Universe, which is unavoidable to contact so long as an organism is present *in* the Physical Universe. But cosmic radiation is only one source of potential "chemical fragmentation" and a minor one at best, since we now have come to discover many greater sources of harmful radiations; either by unearthing them or generating them as byproducts of our industrialization.

Authorities have always gone in their own directions—often inspired by their own political, business and financial-power agendas—concerning any official opinions regarding effects on the *Human Condition*—or even the linger effects of their original and ongoing nuclear tinkering altogether; but this displacement of responsibility only ensures that these problems are certain to be with us for a very long time. The fact is that we are again returning to an era of testing and standoffs regarding the weaponized use of devices that directly **conflict** with the utilitarian ethics of our *Systemology*. It is likely that this is going to have a visible effect on the health of the public condition—including the general state of morale concerning a continuing existence into the future. So long as the *Human Condition* is held suspended in present problems reacted to by past programming, there is little hope for charting an appropriate future to support the most ideal conditions for *Life* to exist; and to be certain that it may continue to go on existing for many generations to come.

On a higher level of understanding, the issues of *nuclear* and *electromagnetic* "radiation" and other cumulative *toxins* and *chemical* sources of fragmentation all contribute toward a reduction in health and *Awareness* for the *Human Condition.* Contact with and absorption of many components found in our "modern" world are "contagions" for illness for those who are consistently exposed or chronically maintain lower ZU frequencies. One reason is that all forms of *fragmentation* are cumulative in effect—stored and carried over the entire lifetime of an individual, with many aspects even carried over into multiple lifetimes.

As a holistic approach to understanding and managing the fundamentals of the *Human Condition*, there are factors to consider that extend even beyond physical nature of radiation itself. There is the general condition of "mental health" and "spiritual wellbeing" to consider, regarding a population held in emotional paralysis by one source or another, promoting everything from general worry to blatant hysteria. All of these states and conditions serve only to reinforce positions of uncertainty on the part of the individual—especially when we are said to be a part of a group, a society, a nation or a race and we haven't the foggiest clue of why things are going on in our name. This also successfully fragments the individual, the group, the society, nation and race—all at once.

And this is what we are here to learn to resolve; this is what the fundamentals of *Systemology* reveal when applied to the world around us. We are starting with the individual and bringing them to an increased capacity for ability that will lead us to a true continued existence that is *Self-Honest* and true; not just true for one—but true for all. And this level of truth *is* very much attainable in this existence—during this lifetime—no matter what anyone has said to you.

You can *know*. You can *do*. And you can *be*. And I believe we are off to the right start if anything that I have said in these preliminary articles has been found effective for you, or inspiring to you, in generating the momentum of that first step forward in this direction. There are many more aspects to *Mardukite Zuism* and *NexGen Systemology*—many new vistas and discoveries that can be shared with you; but for now, I would like to leave you with these kernels that have been put forth, in hopes that these few small seeds will germinate into something real that you can grasp, so that when you come back looking to know the rest, you will not have to know it on *faith* and *trust*; you will be able to recognize that it is true and real, because you will *know* that it is true and real. You will know for yourself, because you know yourself. I am simply here holding a door open for you. So just mind the gap and pass through. You have friends waiting to welcome you on the other side.

THE ARCANE KNOWLEDGE FROM MARDUK'S TABLET OF DESTINY.*

1.) As above, so below; On earth as it is in Heaven
an-bala ki-bala an-ba ki an-ba

2.) What the Mind believes, the Spirit reinforces
da-ga nam-ku-zu dingir-Lamma a bi-ib-gar

3.) When disaster is self-made, no man can interfere
nig-ku-lam-ma dingir-ra-na-ka su—tu-tu nu-ub-zu

4.) What is given in submission is a catalyst for defiance
nig-gu-gar-ra nig-gaba-gar-ra

5.) Whoever partners with Truth, creates Life
nig-ge-na-ta a-ba in-da-di nam-ti i-u-tu

---

* Excerpted from *"The Tablets of Destiny"* by Joshua Free.

ARCANE KNOWLEDGE FROM THE ANUNNAKI TABLET OF UNION.*

All Life is precious for the fact that it lives.
Life *IS* – existing against all odds,
And Life grows and develops following a course.
Love is Will – and Love creates Emotion.
Love is everything in this world.
God is the Supreme Being,
That which represents True Pure All-Powerful Love,
The Light that binds and unites the Universe
In its Creation and Destruction.

God is the conscience at the center of all Life.
When you put Love and Light into Life, which is God,
The Spirit of that Life is Eternal.
The "Devil" is a name given to the path that leads
To harming one another and the Self
Against the Natural Order,
And promoting the belief that one can live without Love.
You cannot exist without Love.

Love is even in what is considered "Evil," for it to exist.
As the Love in "Evil" manifests the Demons of Jealousy,
Demons of Misery, Greed, Pain and Grief.

The Power to Create is in Love
And the Power to Destroy is in Love.
To live for yourself alone outside of Love
Is union with Greed.

As the Love of God is in all Life,
The Natural State of Unity in all Life
IS to Love all Life.

---

* Excerpted from *Mardukite Tablet-R (2009)*; reprinted in *Complete Anunnaki Bible* edited by Joshua Free.

NEXGEN SYSTEMOLOGY GLOSSARY*

A-for-A (one-to-one) : meaning that what we say, write, represent, think or symbolize is a direct and perfect reflection of the actual aspect or thing—that "A" is for, means and is equivalent to "A" and not "a" or "q" or "!"

aberration : a deviation from, or distortion in, what is true or right or straight.

acknowledgment : a response-communication establishing that an immediately former communication was properly received, duplicated and understood; the formal acceptance and/or recognition of a communication or presence.

actualization : to make actual; to bring into Reality; to realize fully in *Awareness*.

affinity : the apparent and energetic *relationship* between substances or bodies; the degree of *attraction* or repulsion between things based on natural forces; the *similitude* of frequencies or waveforms; the degree of *interconnection* between systems.

agreement : unanimity of opinion; an accepted arrangement; "reality."

allegorical : a representation of the abstract, metaphysical or "spiritual" using physical or concrete forms.

alpha : the first, primary, basic, superior or beginning of some form; in NexGen systemology, it also refers to the state of existence that operates on archetypes, will and intention "exterior" to the low-level condensation and solidarity of energy and matter as the 'physical universe'.

alpha-spirit : a "spiritual" *Life*-form; the "true" *Self* or I-AM; the spiritual (*alpha*) *Self* that is animating the (*beta*) physical body or "*genetic vehicle*" using a continuous *Lifeline* of spiritual ("*ZU*") energy; an individual spiritual (*alpha*) entity possessing no physical mass or measurable waveform (motion) in the Physical Universe as itself, so it animates the (*beta*) physical

* Excerpted from *NexGen Systemology Glossary v.4.2*; only those words which appear in this present volume are included.

body or "*genetic vehicle*" as a catalyst to experience *Self*-determined causality in effect within the *Physical Universe*.

AN : an ancient cuneiform sign designating the *'spiritual zone'*; the *Spiritual Universe*—comprised of spiritual matter and spiritual energy; a direction of motion toward spiritual *Infinity*, away from or superior to the physical (*'KI'*); the spiritual condition of existence providing for our primary *Alpha* state as an individual *Identity* or *I-AM-Self* which interacts and experiences *Awareness* of a *beta* state in the *Physical Universe* ('*KI*') as *Life*.

anathema : a thing or person to be detested, loathed or avoided; a thing or person accursed or despised such as to wish damnation or "divine punishment" upon.

anchor (*conceptual*) : a stable point in space; a fixed point used to hold or stabilize a spatial existence of other points; a spatial point that fixes the parameters of dimensional orientation, such as the corner-points of a solid object in relation to other points in space; in *NexGen Systemology*, "beta-anchored" is an expression used to describe the fixed orientation of a viewpoint from Self in relation to all possible spatial points in *beta-existence* ("physical universe"), or else the existential points that fix the operation of the "body" within the space-time of *beta-existence*.

Ancient Mystery School : the original arcane source of all esoteric knowledge on Earth, concentrated between the Middle East and modern-day Turkey and Transylvania c. 6000 B.C. and then dispersing south (Mesopotamia), west (Europe) and east (Asia) from that location.

apparent : visibly exposed to sight; evident rather than actual, as presumed by Observation; readily perceived, especially by the senses.

archetype : a "first form" or ideal conceptual model of some aspect; the ultimate prototype of a form on which all other conceptions are based.

ascension : actualized *Awareness* elevated to the point of true "spiritual existence" exterior to *beta existence*. An "Ascended Master" is one who has returned to an incarnation on Earth as an inherently *Enlightened One*, demonstrable in their actions—they have the ability to *Self-direct* the "Spirit" as *Self*, just as we are treating the "Mind" and "Body" at this current grade of instruction; in *Moroii ad Vitam*, a state of Beingness after *First Death*, experienced by an *etheric body*, which is able to maintain consciousness as a personal identity continuum with the same *Self-directed* control and communication of Will-Intention that is exercised, actualized and developed deliberately during one's present incarnation.

assessment scale : an official assignment of graded/gradient numeric values.

associative knowledge : significance or meaning of a facet or aspect assigned to (or considered to have) a direct relationship with another facet; to connect or relate ideas or facets of existence with one another; a reactive-response image, emotion or conception that is suggested by (or directly accompanies) something other than itself; in traditional systems logic, an equivalency of significance or meaning between facets or sets that are grouped together, such as in $(a + b) + c = a + (b + c)$; in NexGen Systemology, erroneous associative knowledge is assignment of the same value to all facets or parts considered as related (even when they are not actually so), such as in $a = a$, $b = a$, $c = a$ and so forth without distinction.

attention : active use of *Awareness* toward a specific aspect or thing; the act of "attending" with the presence of *Self*; a direction of focus or concentration of *Awareness* along a particular channel or conduit or toward a particular terminal node or communication termination point; the Self-directed concentration of personal energy as a combination of observation, thought-waves and consideration.

authoritarian : knowledge as truth, boundaries and freedoms dictated to an individual by a perceived, regulated or enforced "authority."

auto-suggestion (self-hypnosis) : auto-conditioning; self-programming; delivering directed affirmations or statements repeatedly to *Self* in order to condition a change in behavior or beliefs; any *Self-directed* technique intended to generate a specific "*post-hypnotic suggestion.*"

awareness : the highest sense of-and-as Self in knowing and being as I-AM (the *Alpha-Spirit*); the extent of beingness directed as a POV experienced by Self as knowingness.

Babylonian : the Mesopotamian civilization that evolved from *Sumer*; the inception of all societal and religious systematization.

band : a division or group; in *NexGen Systemology*—a division or set of frequencies on the ZU-line that are tuned closely together and referred to as a group.

BAT (Beta-Awareness Test) : a method of *psychometric evaluation* developed for *Mardukite Systemology* to determine a "basic" or "average" state of personal *beta-Awareness.*

beta (existence) : all manifestation in the "Physical Universe" (KI); the "Physical" state of existence consisting of vibrations of physical energy and physical matter moving through physical space and experienced as "time"; the conditions of *Awareness* for the *Alpha-spirit* (*Self*) as a physical organic *Lifeform* or "*genetic vehicle*" in which it experiences causality in the *Physical Universe.*

Biofeedback/biomagnetic : a measurable effect, such as a change in electrical resistance, that is produced by thoughts, emotions and physical behaviors which generate specific 'neurotransmitters' and biochemical reactions in the brain, body and across the skin surface.

capable : the actual capacity for potential ability.

catalog : a systematic list of knowledge or record of data.

catalyst : something that causes action between two systems or aspects, but which itself is unaffected as a variable of this energy communication; a medium or intermediary channel.

catharsis / cathartic processing : from the Greek root meaning "pure" or "perfect"; the emptying out or discharge of emotional stores; practices of "consolamentum" where an individual removes distorting/fragmented emotional charges and encoding from a personal energy flow/circuit and some other terminal, thing, &tc.

causative : as being the cause.

chakra : (an archaic term used by ancient wisdom traditions); an etheric wheel-mechanism that processes *ZU* energy at specific frequencies along the *ZU-line*, of which a Human being reportedly has *seven* at various degrees.

channel : a specific stream, course, direction or route.

charge : to fill or furnish with a quality; to supply with energy; to lay a command upon; in *NexGen Systemology*—to imbue with intention; to overspread with emotion; application of *Self-directed (WILL)* "intention" toward an emotional manifestation in beta-existence; personal energy stores and significances entwined as fragmentation in mental images, reactive-response encoding and intellectual (and/or) programmed beliefs; in traditional mysticism, to intentionally fix an energetic resonance to meet some degree, or to bring a specific concentration of energy that is transferred to a focal point, such as an object or space.

chronologically : concerning or pertaining to "time."

codification : the process of arranging knowledge in a systematic form.

command : in *Metahuman Systemology*, abilities of the Self (I-AM), from its ideal exterior POV as Alpha Spirit, to direct a communication for control that is perfectly duplicated along the ZU-line without fragmentation.

command line : see "*processing command line.*"

communication : successful transmission of information, data, energy (&tc.) along a message line, with a reception of feedback; an energetic flow of intention to cause an effect (or duplication) at a distance; the personal energy moved or acted upon by will or else 'selective directed attention'; the 'messenger action' used to transmit and receive energy across a medium.

condition : an apparent state; circumstances and dynamics that affect the order and function of a system; a series of interconnected requirements, barriers and allowances that must be met; in traditional language, to bring a thing toward a specific, desired or intentional new state (such as in conditioning), though to minimize confusion, *NexGen Systemology* usually treats this with the semantics of imprinting, encoding and programming.

conflict : the opposition of two forces of similar magnitude along the same channel or competing for the same terminal; the inability to duplicate another POV; a thought, intention or communication that is met with an opposing counter-thought or counter-intention that generates an energetic cluster.

confront : to come around in front of; to be in the presence of; to stand in front of, or in the face of; to meet "face-to-face" or "face-up-to."

consciousness : the energetic flow of *Awareness*; the Principle System of *Awareness* that is spiritual in nature, which demonstrates potential interaction with all degrees of the Physical Universe; the *Beingness* component of our existence in *Spirit*; the Principle System of *Awareness* as *Spirit* that directs action in the Mind-System.

consideration : careful analytical reflection of all aspects; deliberation; determining the significance of a "thing" in relation to similarity or dissimilarity to other "things"; evaluation of facts and importance of certain facts; thorough examination of all aspects related to, or important for, making a decision; the analysis of consequences and estimation of significance when making decisions.

continuity : being a continuous whole; a complete whole or "total round of"; the balance of the equation [–120 + 120 = 0, &tc.]

continuum : a continuous *whole*; observing all gradients on a *spectrum*; measuring quantitative variation with gradual transition on a spectrum without demonstrating discontinuity or separate parts.

control (systems) : Communication relayed from an operative center or organizational cluster, which incites new activity elsewhere in a system.

correlating : the relationship between two or more aspects, parts or systems.

correspondence : a direct relationship or correlation; see also "*associative knowledge.*"

Cosmic Law : the "Law" of Nature (or the Physical Universe); the "Law" governing cosmic ordering; often called "Natural Law" in sciences and philosophies that attempt to codify or systematize it.

cosmology : a philosophy defining the origins and structure of the universe.

Cosmos : archaic term for the "physical universe"; implies that chaos was brought into order; includes past "universes" that we occupied.

counter-productive : contrary to the greater purpose; anything which brings *all Life* away from its sustainable goals of *Infinite Existence.*

Crossing the Abyss : to enter the spiritual or metaphysical unknown in "Self-annihilation" to purify the Self and "return to the Source."

cuneiform : the oldest extant writing from Mesopotamia; wedge-shaped script inscribed on clay tablets with a reed pen.

cuneiform signs : the cuneiform script, as used in ancient Mesopotamia, is not represented in a linear alphabet of "letters," but by a systematic use of basic word "signs" that are combined to form more complex word "signs."

defragmentation : the *reparation* of wholeness; a process of removing "*fragmentation*" in data or knowledge to provide a clear understanding; applying techniques and processes that promote a *holistic* interconnected *alpha* state, favoring observational *Awareness* of continuity in all spiritual and physical systems; in *NexGen Systemology*, a "*Seeker*" achieving an actualized state of basic "*Self-Honest Awareness*" is said to be *defragmented.*

degree : a physical or conceptual *unit* (or point) defining the variation present relative to a *scale* above and below it; any stage or extent to which something *is* in relation to other possible positions within a *set* of "*parameters*"; a point within a specific range or spectrum; in *NexGen Systemology*, a *Seeker's* potential energy variations or fluctuations in thought, emotional reaction and physical perception are all treated as "*degrees.*"

demographics : identifying segments of the population, real or representative.

destiny : what is set down, made firm, standard, or stands fixed as a constant end; the absolute *destination* regardless of whatever course is traveled; in *NexGen Systemology*, the "*des-*

tiny" of the "*Human Spirit*" (or "*Alpha Spirit*") is infinite existence—"*Immortality.*"

dichotomy : a division into two parts, types or kinds.

differentiation : an apparent difference between aspects or concepts.

discernment : to perceive, distinguish and/or differentiate experience into true knowledge.

displace : to compel to leave; to move or replace something with something else in its place or space.

dross : prime material; specifically waste-matter or refuse; the discarded remains collected together.

dynamic (systems) : a principle or fixed system which demonstrates its *'variations'* in activity (or output) only in constant relation to variables or fluctuation of interrelated systems; a standard principle, function, process or system that exhibits *'variations'* and change simultaneously with all connected systems.

Eastern traditions : the evolution of the *Ancient Mystery School* east of its origins, primarily the Asian continent, or what is archaically referred to as "oriental."

echelon : a level or rung on a ladder; a rank or level of command.

emotional encoding : the substance of *imprints*; associations of sensory experience with an *imprint*; perceptions of our environment that receive an *emotional charge*, which form or reinforce facets of an *imprint*; perceptions recorded and stored as an *imprint* within the "emotional range" of energetic manifestation; the formation of an energetic store or charge on a channel that fixes emotional responses as a mechanistic automation, which is carried on in an individual's spiritual timeline or personal continuum of existence.

enact : to make happen; to bring into action; to make part of an act.

encompassing : to form a circle around, surround or envelop around.

enforcement : the act of compelling or putting (effort) into force; to compel or impose obedience by force; to impress strongly with applications of stress to demand agreement or validation; the lowest-level of direct control by physical effort or threat of punishment; a low-level method of control in the absence of true communication.

entropy : the reduction of organized physical systems back into chaos-continuity when their integrity is measured against space over time.

epicenter : the point from which shock-waves travel.

erroneous : inaccurate; incorrect; containing error.

esoteric : hidden; secret; knowledge understood by a select few.

etching : to cut, bite or corrode with acid to produce a pattern.

evaluate : to determine, assign or fix a set value, amount or meaning.

existence : the *state* or fact of *apparent manifestation*; the resulting combination of the Principles of Manifestation: consciousness, motion and substance; continued *survival*; that which independently exists; the *'Prime Directive'* and sole purpose of all manifestation or Reality; the highest common intended motivation driving any "*Thing*" or *Life.*

existential : pertaining to existence, or some aspect or condition of existence.

extant : in existence; existing.

exoteric : public knowledge or common understanding; the level of understanding and *Knowing* maintained by the "masses"; the opposite of *esoteric.*

experiential data : accumulated reference points we store as memory concerning our "experience" with Reality.

extrapolate : to make an estimate of the "value" outside of the perceivable range.

facets : an aspect, an apparent phase; one of many faces of something; a cut surface on a gem or crystal; in *NexGen Systemology*—a single perception or aspect of a memory or "*Imprint*"; any one of many ways in which a memory is recorded; perceptions associated with a painful emotional (sensation) experience and "*imprinted*" onto a metaphoric lens through which to view future similar experiences; other secondary terminals that are associated with a particular terminal, painful event or experience of loss, and which may exhibit the same encoded significance as the activating event.

faculties : abilities of the mind (individual) inherent or developed.

fallacy : a deceptive, misleading, erroneous and/or false beliefs; unsound logic; persuasions, invalidation or enforcement of Reality agreements based on authority, sympathy, bandwagon/mob mentality, vanity, ambiguity, suppression of information, and/or presentation of false dichotomies.

fate : what is brought to light or actualized as experience; the actual *course* taken to reach an end, charted end, or final *destination*; in *NexGen Systemology*, the *'fate'* of a *'Human Spirit'* (or *'Alpha Spirit'*) is determined by the choice of course taken to experience *Life*.

flow : movement across (or through) a channel (or conduit); a direction of active energetic motion typically distinguished as either an *in-flow*, *out-flow* or *cross-flow*.

fragmentation : breaking into parts and scattering the pieces; the *fractioning* of wholeness or the *fracture* of a holistic interconnected *alpha* state, favoring observational *Awareness* of perceived connectivity between parts; *discontinuity*; separation of a totality into parts; in *NexGen Systemology*, a person outside a state of *Self-Honesty* is said to be *fragmented*.

game : a strategic situation where the power of choice is employed or affected; a parameter or condition defined by purposes, freedoms and barriers (rules).

genetic memory : the evolutionary, cellular and genetic (DNA) "memory" encoded into a *genetic vehicle* or *living organism* during its progression and duplication (reproduction) over millions (or billions) of years on Earth; in *NexGen Systemology*—the past-life Earth-memory carried in the genetic makeup of an organism (*genetic vehicle*) that is *independent of any* actual "spiritual memory" maintained by the *Alpha Spirit* themselves, from its own previous lifetimes on Earth and elsewhere using other *genetic vehicles* with no direct evolutionary connection to the current physical form in use.

genetic-vehicle : a physical *Life*-form; the physical (*beta*) body that is animated/controlled by the (*Alpha*) *Spirit* using a continuous *Lifeline* (ZU); a physical (*beta*) organic receptacle and catalyst for the (*Alpha*) *Self* to operate "causes" and experience "effects" within the *Physical Universe.*

gnosis : a *Greek* word meaning knowledge, but specifically "true knowledge"; the highest echelon of "true knowledge" accessible (or attained) only by mystical or spiritual faculties whereby actualized realizations are achieved independent of specialized education.

Gnostics : a name meaning "having knowledge" in Greek language (see also *gnosis*); an early sect of Judeo-Christian mysticism from the 1st Century AD emphasizing true knowledge by *Self-Honest* experience of metahuman and spiritual states of beingness, emphasizing defragmentation of "illusion" and the overcoming of material "deception"; an esoteric proto-Systemology organization disbanded by the Roman Church as heretical.

godhood : a divine character or condition; "divinity."

gradient : a degree of partitioned ascent or descent along some scale, elevation or incline; "higher" and "lower" values in relation to one another.

heralded : proclaimed ahead of or prior to; officially announced.

holistic : the examination of interconnected systems as encompassing something greater than the *sum* of their "parts."

Homo Novus : literally, the "new man"; the "newly elevated man" or "known man" in ancient Rome; the man who "knows (only) through himself"; in NexGen Systemology—the next spiritual and intellectual evolution of *homo sapiens* (the "modern Human Condition"), which is signified by a demonstration of higher faculties of *Self-Actualization* and clear *Awareness.*

Human Condition : a standard default state of Human experience that is generally accepted to be the extent of its potential identity (*beingness*)—currently treated as *Homo Sapiens Sapiens,* but which is scheduled for replacement by *Homo Novus.*

humanistic psychology : a field of academic psychology approaching a holistic emphasis on *Self-Actualization* as an individual's most basic motivation; early key figures from the 20th century include: Carl Rogers, Abraham Maslow, L. Ron Hubbard, William Walker Atkinson, Deepak Chopra and Timothy Leary (to name a few).

identity : the collection of energy and matter—including memory—across the "*Spiritual Continuum*" that we consider as "I" of *Self.*

identity-system : the application of the *ZU-line* as "I"—the continuous expression of *Self* as *Awareness.*

imagination : the ability to create imagery in the mind at will and change or alter it as desired; the ability to create, change and dissolve mental images on command or as an act of will; to create a mental image or have associated imagery displayed (or "conjured") in the mind that may or may not be treated as real (or memory recall) and may or may not accurately duplicate objective reality.

imprint : to strongly impress, stamp, mark (or outline) onto a softer 'impressible' substance; to mark with pressure onto a surface; in *NexGen Systemology*, the term is used to indicate permanent Reality impressions marked by frequencies, energies or interactions experienced during periods of emotional distress, pain, unconsciousness, loss, enforcement, or something antagonistic to physical (personal) survival, all of which are are stored with other reactive response-mechanisms at lower-levels of *Awareness* as opposed to the active memory database and proactive processing center of the Mind; an experiential "memory-set" that may later resurface—be triggered or stimulated artificially—as Reality, of which similar responses will be engaged automatically.

imprinting incident : the first or original event instance communicated and *emotionally encoded* onto an individual's "timeline" (their memory of events over the course of one or all lifetimes) that formed a permanent impression that is later used to mechanistically treat future contact on that channel; the first or original occurrence of some particular *facet* or mental image related to a certain type of *encoded response*, such as pain and discomfort, losses and victimization, and even the acts that we have taken against others along the timeline that caused them to also be *Imprinted*.

incarnation : a present, living or concrete form of some thing or idea.

inception : the beginning, start, origin or outset.

individual : a person, lifeform or human entity; a *Seeker* or potential *Seeker* is often referred to as an "individual" within Mardukite Zuism and Systemology materials.

infinite existence : "immortality."

inhibited : withheld, discouraged or repressed from some state.

institution : a social standard or organizational group responsible for promoting some system or aspect in society.

intention : the directed application of Will; to intend (have "in Mind") or signify (give "significance" to) for or toward a particular purpose; in *NexGen Systemology* (from the *Standard Model*)—the spiritual activity at WILL (5.0) directed by an *Alpha Spirit* (7.0); the application of WILL as "Cause" from a higher order of Alpha Thought and consideration (6.0), which then may continue to relay communications as an "effect" in the universe.

invests : spends on; gives or devotes something to earn a result; endows with.

"kNow" : a creative spelling and use of semantics for "know" and "now" to indicate the state of present-time actualized "Awareness" as Self (Alpha-Spirit), developed for fun dual-meaning messages made by early Mardukite Systemologists in 2008-9, such as "live in the kNow" or "be in the kNow" and even "drown in the kNow" &tc.

knowledge : clear personal processing of informed understanding; information (data) that is actualized as effectively workable understanding; a demonstrable understanding on which we may 'set' our *Awareness*—or literally a "know-ledge."

KI : an ancient cuneiform sign designating the *'physical zone'*; the *Physical Universe*—comprised of physical matter and physical energy in action across space and observed as time; a direction of motion toward material *Continuity*, away from or subordinate to the Spiritual (*'AN'*); the physical condition of existence providing for our *beta* state of *Awareness* experienced (and interacted with) as an individual *Lifeform* from our primary Alpha state of Identity or *I-AM-Self* in the *Spiritual Universe* ('*AN*').

kinetic : pertaining to the energy of physical motion and movement.

level : a physical or conceptual *tier* (or plane) relative to a *scale* above and below it; a significant *gradient* observable as a *foundation* (or surface) built upon and subsequent to other levels of a totality or whole; a *set* of "*parameters*" with respect to other such *sets* along a *continuum*; in *NexGen Systemology*, a *Seeker's* understanding, *Awareness* as *Self* and the formal grades of material/instruction are all treated as "*levels*."

localized : brought together and confined to a particular place.

logic equations : using symbols and basic mathematical logic to establish the validity of statements or to see how a variable within a system will change the result; a basic demonstration of proportion or relationship between variables in a system.

logistics : pertaining to the movement or transportation between locations.

manifestation : something brought into existence.

Marduk : founder of Babylonia; patron Anunnaki "god" of Babylon.

Mardukite Zuism : a Mesopotamian-themed (Babylonian-oriented) religious philosophy and tradition applying the spiritual technology based on *Arcane Tablets* in combination with "Tech" from *NexGen Systemology*; first developed in the New Age underground by Joshua Free in 2008 and realized publicly in 2009 with the formal establishment of the "*Mardukite Chamberlains*."

master control center (MCC) : a perfect computing device to the extent of the information received from "lower levels" of sensory experience/perception; the proactive communication system of the "*Mind*"; a relay point of active *Awareness* along the Identity's *ZU-line*, which is responsible for maintaining basic *Self-Honest Clarity* of *Knowingness* as a *seat of consciousness* between the *Alpha-Spirit* and the secondary "*Reactive Control Center*" of a *Lifeform* in *beta existence*; the Mind-center for an *Alpha-Spirit* to actualize cause in the *beta existence*; the analytical *Self-Determined* Mind-center of an *Alpha-Spirit used* to project *Will* toward the genetic body; the point of contact between *Spiritual Systems* and the *beta existence*; presumably the "*Third Eye*" of a being connected directly to the *I-AM-Self*, which is responsible for *determining* Reality at any time; in *NexGen Systemology*, this is plotted at (4.0) on the continuity model of the *ZU-line*.

Mesopotamia : land between Tigris and Euphrates River; modern-day Iraq.

methodology : a system of methods, principles and rules to compose a systematic paradigm of philosophy or science.

"Mind's Eye" : the point where the "mental pictures" (and senses) are generated that define what an individual believes they are experiencing in present time; the activities of the "Third-Eye" (or actualized MCC) where the *Alpha-Spirit* directly interacts with the organic *genetic vehicle* in *beta-existence*; *Self-directed* activity on the plane of "mental consciousness" maintained between "spiritual consciousness" of the *Alpha-Spirit* and the "physical/emotional consciousness" of the *genetic vehicle*; the "consciousness activity" *Self-directed* by an actualized WILL.

misappropriated : put into use incorrectly; to apply ineffectively or as unintended by design.

motor functions : internal mechanisms that allow a body to move.

Nabu : the original "god of wisdom, writing and knowledge." (Babylonian)

neurotransmitter : a chemical substance released at a physiological level (of the genetic vehicle) that bridges communication of energetic transmission between the *Mind-Body* systems, using the "nervous system" of the physical body; biochemical amino acids and peptides (neuropeptides), hormones, &tc.

NexGen Systemology : a modern tradition of applied religious philosophy and spiritual technology based on *Arcane Tablets* in combination with "*general systemology*" and "*games theory*" developed in the New Age underground by Joshua Free in 2011 as an advanced futurist extension of the "*Mardukite Chamberlains.*"

objectively : concerning the "external world" and attempts to observe Reality independent of personal "subjective" factors.

optimum : the most favorable or ideal conditions for the best result; the greatest degree of result under specific conditions.

orchestration : to arrange or compose the performance of a system.

organic : as related to a physically living organism or carbon-based life form; energy-matter condensed into form as a focus or POV of Spiritual Life Energy (*ZU*) as it pertains to beta-existence of *this* Physical Universe (*KI*).

paradigm : an all-encompassing *standard* by which to view the world and *communicate* Reality; a standard model of reality-systems used by the Mind to filter, organize and interpret experience of Reality.

parameters : a defined range of possible variables within a model, spectrum or continuum; the extent of communicable reach capable within a system or across a distance; the defined or imposed limitations placed on a system or the functions within a system; the extent to which a Life or "thing" can *be*, *do* or *know* along any channel within the confines of a specific system or spectrum of existence.

paramount : the most important; "above all else."

participation : being part of the action or affecting the result.

patterns (probability patterns) : observation of cycles and tendencies to predict a causal relationship or determine the actual condition or flow of dynamic energy using a holistic systemology to understand Life, Reality and Existence as opposed to isolating or excluding perceived parts as being mutually separate from other perceived parts.

personality (program) : the total composite picture an individual "identifies" themselves with; the accumulated sum of material and mental mass by which an individual experiences as their timeline; a "beta-personality" is mainly attached to the identity of a particular physical body and the total sum of its own genetic memory in combination with the data stores and pictures maintained by the Alpha Spirit; a "true personality" is the Alpha Spirit as Self completely defragmented of all erroneous limitations and barriers to consideration, belief, manifestation and intention.

perturbation : the deviation from a natural state, fixed motion, or orbit system caused by another external system; disturbing or disquieting the serenity of an existent state; inciting observable apparent action using indirect or outside actions or 'forces'; the introduction of a new element or facet that disturbs equilibrium of a standard system; the "butterfly effect"; in *NexGen Systemology*, *'perturbation'* is a necessary condition for the *ZU-line* to function as a *Standard Model* of actual *'monistic continuity'*—which is a *Lifeforce* singularity expressed along a spectrum with potential interactions at each degree from any source; the influence of a degree in one state by activities of another state that seem independent, but which are actually connected directly at some higher degree, even if not apparently observed.

phase : in *NexGen Systemology,* a pattern of personality or identity that is assumed as the POV from *Self*; see also "*phase alignment.*"

phase alignment or "***in phase***" : to be in synch, in step or aligned properly with something else in order to increase the total strength value; in *NexGen Systemology*—referring to alignment of *Awareness* with a particular identity, space or time (such as being *in* Self *in* present *space* and *time*).

physics : a science of motions, forces and bodies in the Physical Universe.

physiology : a science of motions of living bodies or organisms.

pilfering : to steal in small quantities; petty theft.

pilot : the steersman of a ship; in *NexGen Systemology*—an individual qualified to operate *Systemology Processing* for other *Seekers* on the *Pathway to Self-Honesty*.

point-of-view (POV) : an opinion or attitude as expressed from a specific identity-phase; a specific standpoint or vantage-point; a definitive manner of consideration specific to an individual phase or identity; a place or position affording a specific view or vantage; circumstances and programming of an individual that is conducive to a particular response, consideration or belief-set (paradigm); a position (consideration) or place (location) that provides a specific view or perspective (subjective) on experience (of the objective).

postulate : to put forward as truth; to suggest or assume an existence *to be*; to provide a basis of reasoning and belief; a basic theory accepted as fact.

potentiality : the total "sum" (collective amount) of "latent" (dormant—present but not apparent) capable or possible realizations; used to describe a state or condition of what has not yet manifested, but which can be influenced and predicted based on observed patterns and, if referring to beta-existence, Cosmic Law.

precedent : a matter which precedes or goes before another in importance.

premise : a basis or statement of fact from which conclusions are drawn.

prevalent : of wide extent; an extensive or largely accepted aspect or current state.

"process-out" or **"flatten a wave"** : to reduce *emotional encoding* of an *imprint* to zero; to dissolve a *wave-form* or *thought-formed* "solid" such as a "*belief*"; to completely run a *process* to its end, thereby *flattening* any previously "*collapsed-waves*" or *fragmentation* that is obstructing the *clear channel* of *Self-Awareness*; also referred to as "processing-out"; to discharge all previously held emotionally encoded imprinting or erroneous programming and beliefs that otherwise fix the free flow (wave) to a particular pattern, solid or concrete "*is*" form.

processing, systematic : the inner-workings or "through-put" result of systems; in *NexGen Systemology*, a methodology of applied spiritual technology used toward personal Self-Actualization; methods of selective directed attention, communicated language and associative imagery that targets an increase in personal control of the human condition.

processing command line (PCL) or **command line** : a directed input; a specific command using highly selective language for *Systemology Processing*; a predetermined directive statement (cause) intended to focus concentrated attention (effect).

proportional : having a direct relationship or mutual interaction with.

Proto-Indo-European (PIE) : a single source root language c.4500 B.C. contributing to most European languages.

psychometric evaluation : the relative measurement of personal ability, mental (psychological/thought) faculties, and effective processing of information and external stimulus data; a scale used in "applied psychology" to evaluate and predict human behavior.

reactive control center (RCC) : the secondary (reactive) communication system of the "*Mind*"; a relay point of *Awareness* along the Identity's *ZU-line*, which is responsible for engaging basic motors, biochemical processes and any *programmed automated responses* of a living *beta* organism; the reactive Mind-Center of a living organism relaying communications of *Awareness* between causal experience of *Physical Systems* and the "*Master Control Center*"; it presumably stores all emotional encoded imprints as fragmentation of "chakra" frequencies of *ZU* (within the range of the "*psychological/emotive systems*" of a being), which it may *react* to as Reality at any time; in *NexGen Systemology*, this is plotted at (2.0) on the continuity model of the *ZU-line*.

realization : the clear perception of an understanding; to make "real" or give "reality" to so as to grant a property of "beingness" or "being as it is"; the state or instance of coming to an *Awareness*; in *NexGen Systemology*, "gnosis" or true knowledge achieved during *systematic processing*; achievement of a new (or "higher") cognition, true knowledge or perception of Self in relation to reality.

receptacle : a device or mechanism designed to contain and store a specific type of aspect or thing; a container meant to receive something.

recursive : repeating by looping back onto itself to form continuity; *ex.* the "Infinity" symbol is recursive.

relative : an apparent point, state or condition treated as distinct from others.

responsibility : the *ability* to *respond*; the extent of mobilizing *power* and *understanding* an individual maintains as *Awareness* to enact *change*; the proactive ability to *Self-direct* and make decisions independent of an outside authority.

resurface : to return to, or bring up to, the "surface" what has been submerged; in *NexGen Systemology*—relating specifically to processes where a *Seeker* recalls blocked energy stored covertly as emotional "*imprints*" (by the RCC) so that it may be effectively defragmented from the "*ZU-line*" (by the MCC).

Seeker : an individual on the *Pathway to Self-Honesty*; a practitioner of *Mardukite Systemology* or *NexGen Systemology Processing* that is working toward *Ascension.*

Self-actualization : bringing the full potential of the Human spirit into Reality; expressing full capabilities and creativeness of the *Alpha-Spirit.*

Self-determinism : the freedom to act, clear of external control or influence; the personal control of Will to direct intention.

Self-honesty : the *alpha* state of *being* and *knowing*; clear and present total *Awareness* of-and-as *Self*, in its most basic and true proactive expression of itself as *Spirit* or *I-AM*—free of artificial attachments, perceptive filters and other emotionally-reactive or mentally-conditioned programming imposed on the human condition by the systematized physical world.

semantics : the *meaning* carried in *language* as the *truth* of a "thing" represented, *A-for-A*; the *effect* of language on *thought* activity in the Mind and physical behavior; language as *symbols* used to represent a concept, "thing" or "solid."

semantic-set : the implied meaning behind any groupings of words or symbols used to define a specific paradigm.

sentient : consciously intelligent.

simulacrum : an tangible image, facsimile or superficial representation that carries a likeness or similarity to someone or something else; in *NexGen Systemology*—the *genetic vehicle* or physical body is an example of a "simulacrum" of the true *Al-*

pha-Spirit or *Self* (I-AM), which otherwise has no tangible form in *beta-existence.*

singularity : a point where apparently dissimilar qualities of all aspects share a singular expression, nature or quality.

slate : a flat surface used for writing on; a chalk-board.

space : the viewpoint (or POV) extended out from any point out toward a dimension or dimensions; the consideration of a point or spot; the field of energy/matter mass created as a result of communication and control in action and measured as time (wave-length).

spectrum : a broad range or array as a continuous series or sequence; defined parts along a singular continuum.

standard model : a fundamental *structure* or symbolic construct used to evaluate a complete *set* in *continuity* relative to itself and variable to all other *dynamic systems* as graphed or calculated by *logic*; in *NexGen Systemology*—our existential and cosmological cabbalistic model; a "*monistic continuity model*" demonstrating *total system* interconnectivity "above" and "below" observation of any apparent *parameters*; the *ZU-line* represented as a singular vertical (*y*-axis) waveform in space across dimensional levels (universes) without charting any specific movement across a dimensional time-graph *x*-axis.

static : characterized by a fixed or stationary condition; having no apparent change, movement or fluctuation.

sub-zones : at ranges "below" which we are representing or which is readily observable for current purposes.

successively : what comes after; forward into the future.

succumb : to give way, or give in to, a relatively stronger superior force.

Sumerian : ancient civilization of *Sumer*, founded in Mesopotamia c. 5000 B.C.

superfluous : excessive; unnecessary; needless.

superstition : knowledge accepted without good reason.

sympathy : a sensation, feeling or emotion—of anger, fear, sorrow and/or pity—that is a *personal reaction* to the misfortune and failure of another being.

systematization : to arrange into systems; to systematize or make systematic.

terminal (node) : a point, end or mass on a line; a point or connection for closing an electric circuit, such as a post on a battery terminating at each end of its own systematic function; any end point or 'termination' on a line; a point of connectivity with other points; in systems, any point which may be treated as a contact point of interaction; anything that may be distinguished as an 'is' and is therefore a 'termination point' of a system or along a flow-line which may interact with other related systems it shares a line with; a point of interaction with other points.

thought-experiment : from the German, *Gedankenexperiment*; logical *considerations* or mental models used to concisely visualize consequences (cause-effect sequences) within the context of an imaginary or hypothetical scenario; using faculties of the Mind's Eye to *Imagine* things accurately with *considerations* that *have not* already been consciously experienced in *beta-existence*.

thought-form : apparent *manifestation* or existential *realization* of *Thought-waves* as "solids" even when only apparent in Reality-agreements of the Observer; the treatment of *Thought-waves* as permanent *imprints* obscuring *Self-Honest Clarity* of *Awareness* when reinforced by emotional experience as actualized "thought-formed solids" ("*beliefs*") in the Mind.

threshold : a doorway, gate or entrance point; the degree to which something is to produce an effect within a certain state or condition; the point in which a condition changes from one to the next.

thwarted : to successfully oppose or prevent a purpose from actualizing.

tier : a series of rows or levels, one stacked immediately before or atop another.

time : observation of cycles in action; motion of a particle, energy or wave across space; intervals of action related to other intervals of action as observed in Awareness; a measurable wave-length or frequency in comparison to a static state; the consideration of variations in space.

timeline : plotting out history in a linear (line) model to indic ate instances (experiences) or demonstrate changes in state (space) as measured over time; a singular conception of continuation of observed time as marked by event-intervals and changes in energy and matter across space.

tipping point : a definitive "point" when a series of small changes (to a system) are significant enough to be *realized* or *cause* a larger, more significant change; the critical "point" (in a system) beyond which a significant change takes place or is observed; the "point" at which changes that cross a specific "threshold" reach a noticeably new state or development.

transhumanism : concerning the next evolved state of the "Human Condition," which is to say either in a direction of "internal" or "spiritual" technologies that advance the *Self*, or the direction of "external" and "physical" technologies that either modify or eliminate the *Body*. In our present state of society, it is the "physical" that is selectively *sold* to the masses so that only a select few may experience the "former"; in *NexGen Systemology*, also referred to as "metahumanism" with an emphasis on "spiritual technologies" as opposed to "external" ones.

transmit : to send forth data along some line of communication.

traumatic encoding : information received when the sensory faculties of an organism are "shocked" into learning it as an "emotionally" encoded "*Imprint*."

turbulence : a quality or state of distortion or disturbance that creates irregularity of a flow or pattern; the quality or state of aberration on a line (such as ragged edges) or the emotional "turbulent feelings" attached to a particular flow or terminal node; a violent, haphazard or disharmonious commotion (such as in the ebb of gusts and lulls of wind action).

unconscious : a state when *Awareness* as *Self* is removed from the equation of *Life* experience, though it continues to be recorded in lower-level response mechanisms (fixed to a simulacrum or genetic vehicle) for later retrieval.

undefiled : to remain intact, untouched or unchanged; to be left in an original "virgin" state.

understanding : a clear 'A-for-A' duplication of a communication as 'knowledge', which may be comprehended and retained with its significance assigned in relation to other 'knowledge' treated as a 'significant understanding'; the "grade" or "level" that a knowledge base is collected and the manner in which the data is organized and evaluated.

validation : the reinforcement of agreements of Reality.

vibration : effects of motion or wave-frequency as applied to any system.

vizier : a high ranking official; a minister-of-state.

Western Civilization : the modern history, culture, ideals, values and technology, particularly of Europe and North America as distinguished by growing urbanization and industrialization and born from a rebellion to strong religious indoctrination.

will *or* **WILL** (5.0) : in *NexGen Systemology* (from the *Standard Model*)—the spiritual ability at (5.0) of an *Alpha Spirit* (7.0) to apply *intention* as "Cause" from a higher order of reasoning and consideration (6.0) than the thoughts found in *beta-existence,* where it manifests as "effect" below (4.0).

willingness : the ability and consideration to reach, face or confront some thing or energy; the ability and consideration to communicate along some line to produce an effect, to put attention or intention on the line.

ziggurat : ancient Mesopotamian temples in the form of a stepped pyramidal tower presented as a series of seven tiers, levels or terraces.

ZU : the ancient cuneiform sign designating an archaic verb —"*to know,*" "*knowingness*" or "*awareness*"; the active energy/matter of the "Spiritual Universe" (AN) that is experienced as *Lifeforce* or *consciousness* for entities existing in the "Physical Universe" (KI); "*Spiritual Life Energy*"; the spiritual energy present in the WILL of the actualized *Alpha-Spirit* in the "Spiritual Universe" (AN), which imbues its *Awareness* into the Physical Universe (KI), animating/controlling *Life* for its experience of *beta-existence* along an *Identity-continuum* called a *ZU-line.*

Zu-line : a spectrum of *Spiritual Life Energy (ZU)* as conceived on the Standard Model of Systemology; an energetic channel of

Identity-continuum connecting the *Awareness (ZU)* of an *Alpha-Spirit* with "*Infinity*"; a *Life-line* on which *Awareness (ZU)* extends from the direction of the "Spiritual Universe" (AN) as its *alpha state* through an entire possible range of activity in its *beta state*, experienced as a *genetic-entity* occupying the *Physical Universe (KI)*; the Standard Model demonstrates the Zu-line interacting with spheres of existence.

AVAILABLE FROM THE **JOSHUA FREE** PUBLISHING IMPRINT

SYSTEMOLOGY

The Pathway to Self-Honesty

THE ORIGINAL UNDERGROUND CLASSICS

SYSTEMOLOGY: THE ORIGINAL THESIS

An Introduction to 21st Century New Thought

by Joshua Free

(*Mardukite Systemology Liber-S-1X*)

The very first underground discourses released to the "New Thought" division of the Mardukite Research Organization privately over a decade ago and providing the inspiration for rapid futurist spiritual technology called "Mardukite Systemology."

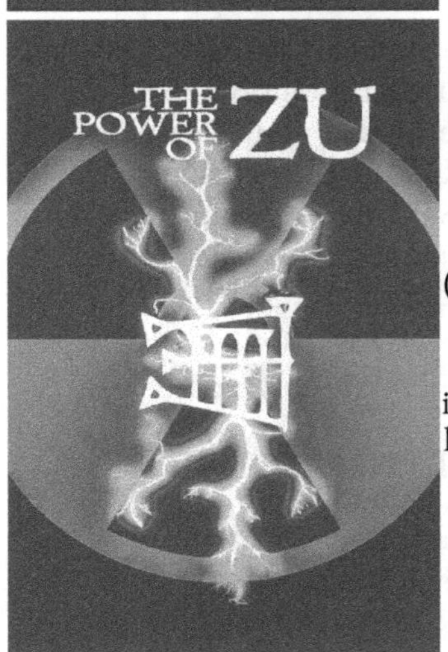

THE POWER OF ZU

Applying Mardukite Zuism & Systemology to Everyday Life

by Joshua Free

Foreword by Reed Penn

(*Mardukite Systemology Liber-S-1Z*)

A unique introductory course on Mardukite Zuism & Systemology, including transcripts from a 3-day lecture series given by Joshua Free in December 2019 to launch the Mardukite Academy of Systemology & Founding Church of Mardukite Zuism just in time for the 2020's.

SYSTEMOLOGY

The Gateways to Infinity

METAHUMAN DESTINATIONS

Piloting the Course to Homo Novus

by Joshua Free
Foreword by David Zibert

Mardukite Systemology Liber-Two

available in hardcover

Drawing from the Arcane Tablets and nearly a year of additional research, experimentation and workshops since the introduction of applied spiritual technology and systematic processing methods, Joshua Free provides the ground-breaking manual for those seeking to correct—or "defragment"—the conditions that have trapped viewpoints of the Spirit into programming and encoding of the Human Condition.

Experience the revolutionary professional course in advanced spiritual technology for Mardukite Systemologists to "Pilot" the way to higher ideals that can free us from the Human Condition and return ultimate command and control of creation to the Spirit.

IMAGINOMICON

The Gateway to Higher Universes

A Grimoire for the Human Spirit

by Joshua Free

Mardukite Systemology Liber-3D

available in hardcover

The Way Out. Hidden for 6,000 Years.
But now we've found the Key.
A grimore to summon and invoke, command and control,
the most powerful spirit to ever exist.
Your Self.

Access beyond physical existence.
Fly free across all Gateways.
Go back to where it all began and reclaim that
personal universe which the *Spirit* once called "*Home.*"

Break free from the Matrix;
command the Mind and control the Body
from outside those systems
— because *You* were never "human" —
fully realize what it means to be a *spiritual being*,
then rise up through the Gateways to Higher Universes
and *BE.*

THE COMPLETE BOOK OF MARDUK BY NABU

A Pocket Anunnaki Devotional Companion to Babylonian Rituals

edited by Joshua Free

10th Anniversary
Collector's Edition Hardcover
Mardukite Liber-W

THE MAQLU RITUAL BOOK

A Pocket Companion to Babylonian Exorcisms, Banishing Rites & Protective Spells

edited by Joshua Free

10th Anniversary
Collector's Edition Hardcover
Mardukite Liber-M

Original underground classics.
Joshua Free's bestselling
"Druid Trilogy"

DRACONOMICON

The Book of Ancient Dragon Magick

25th Anniversary Hardcover Collector's Edition

by Joshua Free

THE DRUID'S HANDBOOK

Ancient Magick for a New Age

20th Anniversary Hardcover Collector's Edition

by Joshua Free

ELVENOMICON -or- SECRET TRADITIONS OF ELVES AND FAERIES

The Book of Elven Magick & Druid Lore

15th Anniversary Hardcover Collector's Edition

by Joshua Free

All three Grade-I Route-D titles
(...plus additional material...)
now available in the anthology:

Merlyn's Complete Book of Druidism

by Joshua Free

THE MARDUKITE RESEARCH LIBRARY ARCHIVE COLLECTION

AVAILABLE FROM THE **JOSHUA FREE** PUBLISHING IMPRINT

Necronomicon: The Anunnaki Bible : 10th Anniversary Collector's Edition—LIBER-N,L,G,9+W-M+S (*Hardcover*)

Gates of the Necronomicon : The Secret Anunnaki Tradition of Babylon : 10th Anniversary Collector's Edition—LIBER-50,51/52,R+555 (*Hardcover*)

Necronomicon—The Anunnaki Grimoire : A Manual of Practical Babylonian Magick : 10th Anniversary Collector's Edition—LIBER-E,W/Z,M+K (*Hardcover*)

The Complete Anunnaki Bible: A Source Book of Esoteric Archaeology —LIBER-N,L,G,9+W-M+S (*Hardcover and Paperback*)

Anunnaki Bible : The Cuneiform Scriptures—New Standard Zuist Edition : Abridged Pocket Version (*Hardcover & Paperback*)

Sumerian Religion : Introducing the Anunnaki Gods of Mesopotamian Neopaganism : 10th Anniv. Collector's Ed.—LIBER-50 (*Hardcover*)

Babylonian Myth & Magic : Anunnaki Mysticism of Mesopotamian Neopaganism : 10th Anniv. Coll. Ed.—LIBER-51+E (*Hardcover*)

The Complete Book of Marduk by Nabu : A Pocket Anunnaki Devotional Companion to Babylonian Prayers & Rituals : 10th Anniversary Collector's Edition—LIBER-W+Z (*Hardcover*)

The Maqlu Ritual Book : A Pocket Companion to Babylonian Exorcisms, Banishing Rites & Protective Spells : 10th Anniversary Collector's Edition—LIBER-M (*Hardcover*)

Novem Portis: Necronomicon Revelations & Nine Gates of the Kingdom of Shadows : 10th Anniv. Collector's Ed.—LIBER-R+9 (*Hardcover*)

Elvenomicon—or—Secret Traditions of Elves & Faeries : Elven Magick & Druid Lore : 15th Anniv. Collector's Ed.—LIBER-D (*Hardcover*)

Draconomicon : The Book of Ancient Dragon Magick 25th Anniversary Collector's Edition—LIBER-D3 (*Hardcover*)

The Druid's Handbook : Ancient Magick for a New Age 20th Anniversary Collector's Edition—LIBER-D2 (*Hardcover*)

The Sorcerer's Handbook : A Complete Guide to Practical Magick 21st Anniversary Collector's Edition—(*Hardcover*)

The Witch's Handbook : A Complete Grimoire of Witchcraft 21st Anniversary Collector's Edition—(*Hardcover*)

The Vampyre's Handbook : Secret Rites of Modern Vampires 5th Anniversary Collector's Edition—LIBER V1+V2 (*Hardcover*)

∞

PUBLISHED BY THE **JOSHUA FREE** IMPRINT REPRESENTING

The Founding Church of Mardukite Zuism
& Mardukite Academy of Systemology

mardukite.com